African Design

'TANDU' SKIN VESSEL AND BATIK DYED CLOTH

AFRICAN DESIGN

Margaret Trowell

PRAEGER PUBLISHERS
New York · Washington

BOOKS THAT MATTER

First published in the United States of America in 1960
by Praeger Publishers, Inc.
111 Fourth Avenue, New York 3, N.Y.
Second edition, 1966
Third edition, 1970
Library of Congress Catalog Card Number : 76–112635

Printed in Great Britain

Contents

Illustrations

There is a map facing page 13

Acknowledgments

Thanks are due to the following museums for permission to reproduce photographs of specimens from their collections:

Cambridge, Museum of Archaeology and Ethnology: XLb.

Dar es Salaam, King George V Museum: XLa.

London, British Museum: Frontispiece, XVc, XVIa, d, XVIIa, b, XVIII, XIXd, XXa, b, XXI, XXIIa, XXVII, XXVIIIa, b, XXIXa, b, XXXIIId, XXXIVa, XXVIa, b, d, XXXVIIIa, b, XXXIXa, b, XLc, d, XLIc, XLIIa, b, c, d, XLIII, XLVIb, La, b, LIa, c, LIIa, b, d, LIIIa, b, c, LVa, LVIIIa, b, LIXc, d, LXIa, b, LXIIa, b, LXIIIb, LXIVa, b, LXVa, b, c, d, LXVIa, b, c, d, LXVIIa, b, c, d, LXVIIIa, b, LXIXa, LXXd, LXXIIb, c, LXXIIIa, c, LXXIVa, LXXV, LXXVIc, d.

Manchester, The University Museum: XXXIIIc, XLIa, b, XLVIa, LXIIIa.

New York, The American Museum of Natural History: LIVc, d, LVI, LXXb.

Oxford, Pitt Rivers Museum: "colour plate facing page 28" XVIb, XVIIc, XXIa, b, c, XXIIb, XXIIIa, b.

Paris, Musée de l'Homme: XXV, XXIXc, XXXIa, b, XXXIIa, b, XXXIIIb, XLVIIa, b, XLVIIIa, b, c, d, XLIXa, b, LVb, LX, LXXIIa.

Tervuren, Musée Royal de l'Afrique Centrale: Xa, b, XIa, b, c, XVb, XVIc, XXIVb, XXVIa, b, XXIXd, XXXIIIa, XXXIVb, XXXVa, d, XXXVIc, XXXVIIa, b, XXXIXc, XLIVb, XLVb, c, LIIc, LIVa, b, LVc, LIXa, b, LXXc, LXXIb, c, d, LXXIIIb, d, LXXIVb, c, d, LXXVIa, b.

Uganda Museum: XIIa, b, XXXVb, c, LIb, LXXa, LXXIa.

Zanzibar, Peace Memorial Museum: XIVa, b.

And to the following writers, publishers and photographers for other photographs:

Plate XLVa is taken from *Afrika, Handbuch de angewandten Volkerkunde* by Univ. Prof. Dr Hugo A. Bernatzik, by kind permission of the author's widow.

Dr P. Bohannan and the Editor of *Man*: XLVd.

The Editor of *Brousse*: IIIb, IVc, IXa.

ACKNOWLEDGEMENTS

Mr H. Cory and Faber and Faber: IIa.

Mr E. H. Duckworth: VI, VII, XXXa, XLIVa.

Mr E. H. Duckworth and the Editor of *Nigeria*: Ia, b, VIIIa, XVa, XXXb, LXIXb.

Mr Gomez: LVIIIc.

Mrs Meyerowitz and Faber and Faber: XXIVa, LXVIIc, d.

Mr P. Moeschlin: LVII.

The Editor of *Nigeria*: IIb.

L'Institut d'Ethnologie, Paris: Va, b.

Mr J. Redinha and the Companhia de Diamantes de Angola: IIIa.

Uganda Information Department: VIIIb.

As is usual in a study of this kind individual thanks are due to far more people than can be mentioned here, among them many members of the staff of the museums listed above. More especially would I thank Miss Bennet-Clark and Mr William Fagg of the British Museum, and Miss Blackwood of the Pitt Rivers Museum; Mrs Ehrlich, Mrs French and Mrs Tattersall for typing the manuscript; the Musée Royal de l'Afrique Centrale for a magnificent gift of photographs of specimens from their collections, many of which are reproduced here; the Council of Makerere College for a research grant and a term of study leave; and last but not least my publishers for the detailed attention and patience which they always give to their publications.

Foreword to the Second Edition

In this second edition of *African Design* the titles of the territories that have become independent since the book was originally published have all been corrected.

With the coming of independence the attention of these countries is naturally focused on social and economic development, and the preservation of the work of the older craftsmen may well be regarded as unnecessary if not retrogressive, for today the emphasis is all on progress.

This, combined with the continual destruction of the craftsmen's work by weathering and insect pests, makes it possible that the traditional skills and natural good taste of the old craftsmen will be forgotten; and the only surviving examples of their work will be found in the showcases of the museums.

Yet good craftsmanship and artistic taste are qualities of which the African peoples have every right to be proud, and which they will surely value highly in the days to come. It is the hope of the writer and publishers of this book that the new edition with its large collection of photographs will stimulate fresh interest in traditional craftsmanship throughout the continent.

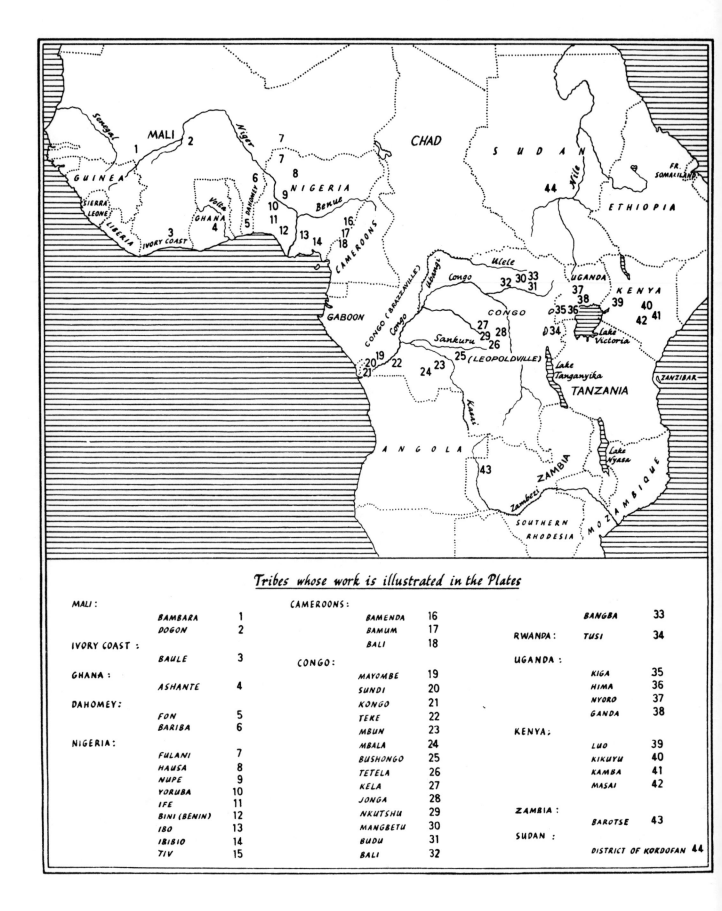

Tribes whose work is illustrated in the Plates

MALI :			CAMEROONS :					
	BAMBARA	1		BAMENDA	16		BANGBA	33
	DOGON	2		BAMUM	17	RWANDA :	TUSI	34
IVORY COAST :				BALI	18			
	BAULE	3	CONGO :			UGANDA :		
GHANA :				MAYOMBE	19		KIGA	35
	ASHANTE	4		SUNDI	20		HIMA	36
DAHOMEY :				KONGO	21		NYORO	37
	FON	5		TEKE	22		GANDA	38
	BARIBA	6		MBUN	23			
NIGERIA :				MBALA	24	KENYA :		
	FULANI	7		BUSHONGO	25		LUO	39
	HAUSA	8		TETELA	26		KIKUYU	40
	NUPE	9		KELA	27		KAMBA	41
	YORUBA	10		JONGA	28		MASAI	42
	IFE	11		NKUTSHU	29			
	BINI (BENIN)	12		MANGBETU	30	ZAMBIA :		
	IBO	13		BUDU	31		BAROTSE	43
	IBIBIO	14		BALI	32	SUDAN :		
	TIV	15					DISTRICT OF KORDOFAN	44

CHAPTER I

The Craftsman's Aim

The 'fine' arts of painting and sculpture have always been considered to be of much greater aesthetic value than the 'applied' arts, by which we mean the various branches of design and ornament applied to the making of our material possessions. In one sense it is good that this should be so, good that even in a material age man instinctively rates higher an activity directed towards a purely aesthetic end rather than towards a purely utilitarian one. But in another sense it is the result of shallow thinking, for if we take the trouble to define our terms and study recognized masterpieces of both fine and applied art we find that both stem from the same roots; man's personal desire to create things of beauty, his need to use his products in the service of his community, and his wish to link himself with the spiritual power or powers behind the visible world through the use or offering of his own small creation.

These intangible urges are obvious in the fine arts but they also exist in the applied ones. We speak of design in a craft, and by that we mean the whole process of planning the shape of an object and its construction in a way which is not only functionally satisfactory but also pleasing to the eye and touch, and this satisfaction is both utilitarian and aesthetic; then we include ornament in design and this element is not in the least essential to the utility of the object but owes its existence solely to the desire of the craftsman and the user for something over and above efficiency and comfort. As for the other considerations which we have suggested above, that is the use of the artist's and craftsman's products for the service of the community and as a link with spiritual powers, here the applied and the so-called fine arts are analogous, both are often commissioned for the service of the social power of the community to enhance its prestige and satisfy its desire for things of beauty, and both may through actual representation or symbolism play an important part in its spiritual and psychological life.

On the other hand the more technical qualities of fitness for purpose and respect for the possibilities and limitations of materials, tools and techniques which are obviously essential for a satisfying design, are really equally important in a painting or a piece of sculpture, though this may not be so obvious to the layman. The difference, then, between a work of fine art and a design for a craft is not absolute but is rather one of emphasis and degree. In a primitive or pre-industrial society even this difference is far less than in a more sophisticated one, for here life is an integrated whole and in both the sculptured ancestor figure and the decorated calabash the practical and the more intangible creative qualities are fairly evenly balanced, for the sculpture is made for the very practical purpose of harnessing spiritual power for material ends, while the decorated calabash has a recognized symbolical significance as well as a material use. The distinction between fine and applied art would puzzle the primitive artist.

We are sometimes apt to designate the craftsmanship of primitive peoples as 'folk art', a term which we use in Western culture for the artistic creations of peasant folk for their own ends. This is somewhat erroneous for although many objects are made by the primitive craftsman for his own household use, yet others such as textiles, food vessels, weapons and wood carving may be created by him for the use of the great chiefs or for special ceremonial purposes within a social system which has, in its own fashion, some resemblance to that which produced the hangings and the furnishings for the Versailles of Louis XIV, and its products will bear the stamp of sophistication of a court art.

The physically controlling factor in the development of all forms of art would seem to be architecture, which is itself largely controlled by the materials available for building. Architecture provides scope and security for all other works of art. Large sculpture, paintings and objects of decorative design are required as a part of the building itself, while smaller portable ones can only be preserved from damage by weather or insects when they are properly housed. The pastoral nomad may have as good an aesthetic sense as his more sedentary brother, indeed in Africa he seems to have that sense more strongly developed than many of the agricultural tribes, but his way of life will give him no encouragement to make large pieces of sculpture or paintings, and even in the decorative crafts he will restrict his skills to weaving, basketry, decorated calabashes and articles of personal adornment rather than heavy, bulky or fragile objects. Among the more sedentary tribes it is those people whose religious customs or social pattern of kingship have led them to develop some form of architecture who have also developed the decorative arts, so that we turn to the West Coast Kingdoms or such people as the Bushongo of the Congo for our best examples of the crafts.

We cannot in fact fit the art of primitive peoples into the exact categories which we use for that of our own society; nevertheless we find that these people, like ourselves, have the fundamental urge to create things of beauty, and through the study of art we must attempt to understand the expression of this common urge in terms of the material and social background of other races and ages. Tradition, fashion, taste and style are all linked to background, as we realize at once when we consider our own art history. We think of the solidity and strength of Romanesque architecture and design which was essential for the life of its time; then of the changes which came through growing technical knowledge and the control of materials as well as the altered social conditions of the later days of Gothic architecture; and, the most striking change of all, of our own day where the combination of vastly increased control of material on the one hand and the lack of servants on the other has created a completely new style of domestic architecture and interior design.

Styles change but the urge is the same. The ladies of Europe in the Middle Ages passed their hours in embroidering wonderful tapestries and hangings for the castle walls. Those of the more cultured tribes of Africa may not have the same wealth of coloured silks at their disposal, but with raffia and vegetable dyes they weave and embroider the finest patterned cloths or make the most delicate basketry. Again in Medieval Europe the monk ornamented the margins of his text with delightful babwyneries and the carver who was employed in building the cathedral decorated the misericords and corbels and waterspouts with the same fantastic types of beasts or with whimsical genre scenes and figures; much of the ivory carving of Benin and wooden panelling of the Yoruba suggests the same approach in the treatment of fabulous reptiles and scenes from everyday life. Heraldry in Europe is paralleled by the appliquéd cloths of Dahomey and Ghana in which the power and might of the chiefs are often expressed by symbolic forms or scenes; while the ceremonial staves and axes and paddles of many African tribes have a refinement and dignity of design which compare favourably with the regalia of more technically advanced peoples in spite of their limited choice of materials. If we are to appreciate the art of a pre-industrial society such as Africa we must study it as a whole, considering the decoration of pots and textiles and wooden vessels as closely as we would the carving of figures and masks. These examples of decorative design may not make the same violent impact on our minds as did African carving on those of Western artists a decade or two ago, but they may well bring fresh vitality to our approach to the purpose and the pleasure of pattern design.

We began by defining design as the whole planning of the shape and construction of an object, using the word in its widest sense, and we should remember that even when the term is used in the more limited field of decoration or ornament it carries with it this wider connotation. By design used in the more restricted sense we mean the decoration of an object such as a wall, panel, pot, basket, vessel or cloth with a pattern in which one or more motifs are repeated in a rhythmical manner; or, if they are not repeated, are fitted together to make a balanced whole within the decorated form. Such patterns are often abstract or geometrical, but representational forms of human, animal or floral types or material objects may be used provided that their treatment is decorative rather than photographic in intention. Such formalized representation is often symbolic.

A study of pattern may be approached in a number of different ways. There is first the technological approach. Working along this line we must study our specimens from the point of view of the possibilities and limitations of the materials and tools which have been used. If the basic material is something hard like stone or metal or wood, or bone or ivory, we shall find it has been carved or engraved, or it may have had other material such as thin sheets of metal appliquéd on to its surface in places, or a contrasting metal or wood or enamel inset, or the whole or part of the object may have been coated with paint. Metal too may be cast, in which case it will be subjected to entirely different treatment.

Clay may be ornamented in a number of different ways, for while it is still soft it may be moulded, or when it is semi-hard it may be impressed or stamped, or engraved or scratched, or later still it may be decorated with a slip of clay of a different colour, or burnished or painted with a coloured glaze.

Fibres again have their appropriate treatment. They may have the pattern woven in the basic structure, or it may be printed on by several different methods, or they may be embroidered with different types of fibre or ornamented by the application of different materials altogether. Each material, whether it be used as the base or as part of the decoration, will give the designer scope for different forms of treatment, and will also have its natural limitations.

Then we must know what kind of tools the artist has used, for these again have their natural possibilities and limitations. An African adze produces a very different surface texture from European carving tools, both have their own beauty and they should never be confused. Again the slight irregularity of handblock printing gives a very different effect from the slick finish of machine printing; both have their place, and a strained effort after mechanical perfection on the part of the handcraftsman is as unpleasant and false as the imitation of irregular handprinting by a machine. Apart from the actual impression of the tool which is used on the material an apparently small variation in technique will open up a whole new range of possible pattern forms.

16

THE CRAFTSMAN'S AIM

From this consideration of materials, tools and techniques we may be tempted to theorize upon matters which are not strictly speaking the concern of the designer. For directly we begin to study the material culture of a people, whether it be the artefacts which they use in everyday life, or the way in which they decorate them, or the non-utilitarian objects which they make for religious or aesthetic purposes, we are at once struck by the pointers which they give us concerning the relationship between one tribe and another. Such and such are the musical instruments of a certain number of tribes; such is the technique used in the basket making of another group, or particular pattern motifs keep cropping up in the ornament of a third set. While it is dangerous to jump to conclusions on flimsy evidence it is at least suggestive that here we have a clue to racial or tribal affinities or a common geographical past.

Then, when we come to study the pattern motifs of these groups more closely in the desire to clarify their apparent similarities and differences, we realize that the whole field of stylization and symbolism is opened before us, and we must study the way in which representational forms, symbols and geometrical pattern are worked out independently from technical considerations. In an inclusive account of the decorative art of Africa both the ethnologist's and the craftsman's approach are equally necessary. A detailed study of the use of the human form in design with all the variations and degrees of stylization which can be found would fill a volume in itself, and the same may be said of any other motif from the whole vocabulary of symbolism. Here little has been attempted beyond discussing the fundamental possibilities and limitations set by technique in applied design, and following it with a description of some pattern forms which seem to be of outstanding interest. The use of human and animal motifs has been illustrated from the work of parts of the West Coast where it seems to be most highly developed; while as the field of geometrical pattern seems to be richest in the Congo our discussion of this type of design has been centred there. The approach is frankly that of an artist rather than of an ethnologist, and makes no pretence of being a detailed survey of the subject. But it has been written in the belief that such an outline would be of interest to the student of art history and to the practical designer, be he African or European.

It has been difficult to decide on the geographical area which should be included in such a study, or to choose a satisfactory title for that area. It would be too big a task to cover the art of the Islamic peoples of North Africa or that of Ethiopia, and it has therefore seemed best to confine the study to what is often termed Africa South of the Sahara, using the term Negro Africa in a very loose sense to cover any African peoples found in that area, and acknowledging definite Moslem influence in the art of such districts as Northern Nigeria and the Coast of East Africa.

B

CHAPTER II

Wall Decoration

ocks and the walls of caves and, as time went on, those of mud huts have presented an attractive surface for decoration since very early times; indeed the earliest two-dimensional art which still exists was carried out on rock walls for, after all, they were the only flat surfaces available. They were painted in earth colours together with soot and perhaps vegetable dyes, so that the colour scheme was restricted to blacks and browns, red and yellow ochres, greys and whites. These rock surfaces had no definitely closed boundary or form, and later the circular wall of a mud hut had little more, so that the sense of necessity for regular pattern was not at first developed, and even today many cave and wall paintings exist in which decorative treatment *per se* is completely lacking. As in all forms of decorative art two trends, the one towards naturalism and the other towards stylization and symbolism, were always at work. On the one hand we find lively and realistic scenes of hunting and battle depicted, on the other we notice forms being reduced to an accepted pictorial shorthand which often seems to have almost no connection with the objects after which the symbols are named. Both representational drawings and symbols are often dotted about the wall surface with no apparent attempt at arrangement. Various techniques are used, the work may be painted, or modelled in low relief in clay, or first modelled and then painted.

It would seem that the initial purpose of both the naturalistic and the symbolic forms used in this way was purely utilitarian. Both had some magico-religious function, and their value for the owner lay in this alone. But man is essentially a creator, and he naturally tends to delight in his creation and to strive after beauty for its own sake. Decoration brings its own discipline, and the artist begins unconsciously to arrange both the representational and symbolic forms within definite panels; he combines the abstract with the realistic to provide borders, or to fill up spaces in the design, and where he uses abstract forms alone he arranges them in an orderly and decorative fashion with due regard to the space which they are intended to fill.

NATURALISTIC MURAL PAINTING
(Plates I, II)

It is in Nigeria that we find the most developed representational mural painting, although it is possible that equally good work may exist in other parts of Africa without having been photographed or recorded. But certainly the large-scale paintings on the walls of Mbari houses, Court houses and chiefs' dwellings in Nigeria are most remarkable for their vitality. Here great stretches of wall are decorated with brightly coloured paintings of scenes from everyday life, broken up by borders and panels of pattern, the works combining realism and decorative quality in a way which is exactly suited to mural painting. The wall paintings by the snake charmers in Tanganyika and those recorded from hut walls in Angola also show the qualities of mural painting in a well-developed form, many of those from Angola most successfully combining stylized human forms with abstract or symbolic pattern.

ABSTRACT DESIGN IN MURAL PAINTING
(Plates III, IV)

In every area where mural painting is practised representational art merges by easy stages into completely abstract pattern or symbolism. A most extraordinarily interesting series of wall paintings have been recorded by Scohy[1] from the village of Ekibondo in the Uele region of the north-east Congo. Here, through the encouragement of an enlightened District Commissioner, a traditional craft of wall painting has been revived and the external hut walls are covered with rich geometrical pattern and panels containing men, animals, fish and other objects. The patterning of the walls is most striking in its boldness and spontaneity.

[1] Scohy, 'Ekibondo'. *Brousse.* 1951, pp. 1–2.

WALL DECORATION
Naturalistic Low Relief Panels in Clay, Wood and Metal
(*Plates V, LVII, LVIII, LXVIII, LXIX*)

Low relief panels in clay, wood and metal, with subjects treated in a naturalistic way, are found in many parts of West Africa. Whether these should be considered as applied design is difficult to decide for although some, through their stylized treatment and emphasis on arrangement, must definitely be regarded in this light, others must be thought of more in sculptural terms. Schmalenbach[1] has pointed out that the sculpture of the African is very largely limited to individual figures. In the more primitive reliefs, too, figures are introduced quite without relationship to one another either by form or pattern, or by any feeling of tension or articulation. As we would say from the angle of this study, there is no sense of design. The first step towards planned design in low relief carving would seem to be shown in the carved door panels of such tribes as the Dogon and Senufo of the Western Sudan, where figures are ranged side by side, or one above the other, in almost military formation; the convention of frontality being adhered to as rigidly as in Byzantine painting. It is only in the work of the coastal kingdoms that more freedom is achieved, and the artist begins to compose his design with a definite sense of rhythm and connection between his units of pattern.

Clay panels in low relief were used to decorate the palace walls of kings and those of the houses of chiefs and juju priests in Dahomey and Nigeria, but the early European explorers with their rigid conventions of representational art found them of little interest. Lander, speaking of some he had seen in Nigeria, says 'the execution, as might be supposed, is rude and contemptible'. Some of the panels from the walls of the royal palaces of Dahomey reproduced by Waterlot[2] are by no means contemptible, but are well-balanced designs, interestingly treated. The bronze plaques of Benin, which covered the walls of the royal palace, have long been some of the best known and most popular forms of African art, chiefly because their air of sophistication and their representation of Portuguese types bring them nearer to our understanding. Whatever their merit, to judge all these explicitly as decorative panels is to use the wrong criteria; although some of them, through their planned arrangement and surface pattern, may be considered in this light. West African low relief carving in wood, used chiefly as door panels but sometimes also set into walls, approaches far more nearly to our definition of design. In these panels the stylized figures of men, beasts, and mythical beings, half-human and half-animal or -reptile, form definite though unsymmetrical

---

[1] Schmalenbach, *African Art*. Macmillan, New York, 1954, p. 154.
[2] Waterlot, *Les Bas-Reliefs des Bâtiments Royaux d'Abomey*. Paris, 1926.

patterns, often contained within bands of geometrical design. In some panels the pattern may consist entirely of interlacing bands or other geometrical motifs.

In both the bronze plaques and the wooden panels the use of small surface pattern gives a richness of texture to the work as a whole. Often the background is practically undecorated, in metal work it may be just relieved by lightly engraved trefoil or quatrefoil forms; in the case of wood the slight unevenness of the tooling prevents monotony; but the figures and other objects represented in relief are a mass of pattern, usually following round the form in bands.

ABSTRACT DESIGN IN MOULDED RELIEF
(Plates VI, VII, VIII)

Moulded pattern, as apart from the naturalistic representation of form, is often found covering the whole surface of external or interior walls and ceilings. In the huts of the Hima of Uganda the motifs used are symbolic, although in many cases their meaning has been forgotten today. These symbols are scattered in a somewhat haphazard fashion over the surface of the wall, but nevertheless produce a pleasing decorative effect with their contrasting colours of red ochre, black and white. On the mud walls of the houses of some parts of Northern Nigeria all types of moulded decoration may be found from pattern wandering across a whole external wall with no suggestion of a repeat, to sets of separate motifs firmly fixed within regular panels.

PAINTED AND MOULDED ORNAMENT ON THE SURFACE OF WALLS AND CEILINGS
(Plate VIII)

The highly ornate vaulted ceiling at Kano illustrated here, is a most advanced example of moulded pattern, and it is interesting to notice the use of coloured china plates inserted as bosses at the junction of the arches. This use of plates or bowls, or even the necks and bottoms of gin bottles sunk deep into the walls so that they appear flush with the surface, is common in many parts of Africa where Moslem influence is strong; such as the Sudan and neighbouring territories to the South, and also the East Coast.

Further use of extraneous material is made by some tribes who construct mosaics of broken pottery and shells, and others who form geometrical patterns with strips of cane set into the wall.

DECORATIVE REED WORK
(*Plate IX*)

A less permanent type of material, but one which is nevertheless used in wall decoration by certain tribes is raffia palm, cane or reed. The Inter-lacustrine Bantu tribes of East Africa lined the walls of their huts and covered the interior supporting pillars of their roofs with reed-work, usually made of cane or elephant grass. These, bound with dark lines of bark, were very decorative, and the work in the houses of chiefs was of a high standard of craftsmanship. The highest development of this craft was to be found in the screens used by the Tusi of Rwanda to partition off that part of the hut where the sacred milk pots were kept. These screens, patterned in black on the natural colour of the reeds, were decorated with a number of traditional symbolic motifs, very largely triangles and zigzags, fitted together in various ways.

The Bushongo, of the Congo, covered both the interior and exterior walls of certain huts with patterned matting. The patterns are geometrical and contain many of the motifs used in the famous pile embroideries of the tribe. It is not clear exactly how this work is done, as Torday and Joyce[1] speak of a frame-work of wood, to which the midribs of raffia palm are fixed horizontally. These are then bound with leaf-fronds, some dyed black, some in natural colour. Van den Bossche,[2] on the other hand, describes the weaving, without a loom, of separate mats, with a warp of mid-rib and weft of twisted cord made from the leaf-fronds; this is woven in twined weave. The finished mat is then fixed into position on the framework.

Thus colour, clay, wood, metal and fibre, all the materials known to a pre-industrial people, were turned to account in the beautifying of the walls of buildings in various parts of Africa. The satisfactory use of any material depends on the understanding which the craftsman has of its possibilities and limitations, for each material has its own peculiarities. That the African craftsman had such an appreciation of appropriate treatment is clear from a study of his varied methods of wall decoration, in which a wider variety of materials and techniques may be used than in any other craft.

[1] Torday and Joyce, 'Les Bushongo'. *Annales du Musée du Congo Belge*. Series III. Tome II. Fasc. I.
[2] Van den Bossche, 'Art Bakuba'. *Brousse* 1952. No. I.

CHAPTER III

Patterns on Mats and Screens

fter our consideration of decorative reed and palm work in the construction
of walls in African huts we come naturally to matting and screens made from
the same materials, for matting fits halfway between these fixed woven partitions and woven textiles. Both the materials and the techniques used are
essentially the same in all three crafts, the materials employed in mat making being
finer and more pliant than those required for partitions, yet less fine and supple than
those used for textiles. This similarity in construction results, as might be expected,
in similarity of pattern. It is, in fact, difficult to draw a hard and fast line between one
craft and another, and for the sake of convenience certain partition screens made by
the Tusi of the Eastern part of the Congo have been illustrated in both this section
and that on wall decoration, while the finely woven raffia mats or cloths of the Central
and Lower Congo have been placed among the textiles. These Congo mats are woven
on a well-developed type of loom, but more usually only the most simple form of frame
is used for holding one set of fibres, and more often than not the work is done with
no loom or frame at all.

Technically speaking the mats of negro Africa seem to fit into three large groups;
there are those which are woven with or without a loom, others which must be described
as sewn rather than woven, and a third class which are made from strips of plaited
palm.

WOVEN MATS
(*Plates X, XI*)

The techniques shortly to be described for textile weaving hold good for woven matting, with the proviso that the mat probably gets harder and rougher wear, so that the strands cannot be safely floated over a large number of others if they are not to be rapidly broken through use. Mats with the warp in one or two colours, and a weft of natural colour, with a large-scale geometrical repeat of a fairly complicated nature are typical of the work of the Lower Congo. Often the work is in plain black or white, at other times rather more colour may be introduced.[1]

Another type of mat from the same area, with animal, bird or human motifs can be most entertaining and attractive. These mats are woven with a warp of white crossed by a weft of black in such a manner that certain large areas appear predominantly white and others black. In this way the shapes of the animals and other motifs are clearly defined either as a black mass, or as a solid form decorated further with small pattern units. Of the three examples shown in Plate XI the first has been included, not because of any merit in the design, but because it shows clearly the technique employed. In both the other two a better sense of design and repetition can be felt, which is especially interesting in the bird pattern.

SEWN MATS
(Plates IX b, X b, XII)

The type I have termed sewn matting has no technical affinity with weaving, but is worked in a similar fashion to coiled basketry. A set of thick rigid splints is sewn together with raffia or some similar material, the fibre passing round the latest splint and piercing the edge of the one below, which is already in place; the stitches being fitted close together so that they completely cover the splint. Almost any type of pattern can be produced in this technique.

The more complicated mat and two screens shown in Plates IXb, and XIIb, also belong to the class of sewn matwork. In the mat the fine parallel splints of the ground are sewn in place by the bands of black pattern. Further interest is given to the design by means of variation in depth, for the pattern is stitched over a fibre cord and so raised like piping in European embroidery.

The screens are examples of the work of the Tusi, which is outstandingly beautiful in its simplicity of design. These people use a comparatively small number of motifs in their mat-making and basketry and restrict their colouring to black on a natural ground, with the occasional addition of a brown. The workmanship is always extremely fine and delicate, and this, together with the quality of the design, gives results of a

---

[1] See *Annales du Musée du Congo Belge*. Series III. Tome II. 'Céramiques et Nattes'.

very high standard. Technically these screens have a woven groundwork of flat splints supporting a patterned covering of black and natural coloured reeds, which are held in place by rows of thin fibre threads twined between each reed. The fastening forms no part of the pattern and is kept as invisible as possible.[1]

PLAITED MATS
(Plates XIII, XIV)

Finally we have plaited matting. Mats of this kind are made by joining together long strips of plaited palm fronds, dyed in various colours. The fronds are finely shredded and any number of strands from six to over fifty may be used in a plait at any one time. The pattern is produced both according to the order in which the different coloured strands are led in from the sides and by the numbering of the opposite strands over and under which they are passed. Each line of plaiting may be made to a different count after the fashion of a knitting pattern. The finished strips are finally sewn together to form a complete mat.[2]

It would seem probable that the craft was introduced into Africa by Arabs from the East, although it has now penetrated many hundreds of miles inland. On the East Coast and the offshore islands it may be seen at its best and gayest, while inland only the most simple patterns are usually found. In a collection of over sixty patterns recently obtained by the writer in Zanzibar the motifs are mostly named according to a fancied or obvious resemblance to a natural object. The Snake, the Bow tie, the Dog's ribs, the Fish, are typical titles. Others such as the Face of the Unmarried Woman, or the Place of the heart, are more exotic. The two prayer mats, also from Zanzibar, illustrated in Plate XIV, are extraordinarily beautiful specimens. The broad strips of pattern would entail working with some fifty strands in the hands, and the irregular pattern formed by the use of Arabic characters in the lower mat would require most skilful counting. The actual design of the upper mat has something of the quality of the design of a Persian rug.

Plaited mat patterns have also found their way into East Africa by a rather different route, being made by the wives of Nubian soldiers from the Sudan. A collection of patterns from Nubian matting is shown in the lower half of Plate XIII. It will be seen that these differ considerably from those shown above them, although in actual fact the difference is only due to one technical change. The Nubian women plait their mats

[1] See Czekanowski, *Forschungen im Nil-Congo- Zwischengebiet.* 1907-8, Vol. II.
[2] See Trowell, *African Arts and Crafts.* Longmans, 1937, pp. 121 et seq.

with a double thickness of strands, working with one colour over another, so that when the end of a plaited line is reached and the strands bent back to be worked in the opposite direction the colours are reversed. The interest of Nubian matting depends on this colour factor rather than on the use of complicated motifs, and one very simple pattern can be found in countless mats worked in various combinations of colour changes.

CHAPTER IV

Textile Design

WOVEN CLOTH
(Plates XV, XVI, XVII, XVIII)

Many early explorers of the West Coast of Africa state that they found the craft of weaving was highly developed there when they arrived. Ling Roth quotes a number of these in early accounts of Benin. First Welsh,[1] one of an English party who went to Benin about 1590, who speaks of 'cloth made of cotton wool very curiously woven and cloth made of barke of the palme trees', and 'The pretie fine mats that they make'.[2] Then an unknown Dutchman, D.R., in 1604 writes of 'much thread spun from cotton, of which they make their clothes similar to those on the Gold Coast, but lighter and finer'.[3] We get a further idea of the extent to which the craft was practised from Nyendal, who in 1704 says, 'not only all the inhabitants are clothed with it, but they annually export thousands of woven cloths to other places',[4] and Landolphe in 1778 writes 'few houses are to be seen without a cotton spinning machine, or frame for making admirable cotton or straw rug'.[5] Then Herskovits[6] quotes a legend which tells of the introduction of weaving into Dahomey in the second half of the seventeenth century by one of the kings, an accepted culture-hero of the tribe. In the Congo, too, the craft was evidently practised from early days, for Pigafetta,[7] writing of the Lower Congo in 1591, speaks of 'garments made from the palm tree of beautiful workmanship'.

[1] Ling Roth, *Great Benin*. Halifax, 1903, p. 131.   [2] Ibid. p. 140.   [3] Ibid. p. 140.   [4] Ibid. p. 141.
[5] Ibid. p. 141.
[6] Herskovits, *Dahomey*. New York, 1938, Vol. I, p. 16.
[7] Filippo Pigafetta. *History of the Kingdom of Congo.* A report of the Kingdom of Congo and surrounding

TEXTILE DESIGN

The weaving of textiles has been practised throughout West Africa, the Congo, and parts of Portuguese East Africa and Tanganyika. It is probable that the technique of weaving on a loom developed from that of mat making without such an apparatus after it had been realized that the work would be much simplified if ways were found, first of fixing all the warp threads at a certain tension so that they neither tangled nor worked loose as the weaving proceeded, and secondly of making sheds or openings through which the shuttle or needle carrying the weft thread could be passed in a more simple fashion than by picking the warp threads up separately each time with the fingers. Various forms of loom are used and these have been described in general by Ling Roth[1] and in more detail in monographs on various tribes. In order to understand the possible range and variety of pattern making on primitive looms such as are used in Africa, a certain amount of technical knowledge of weaving is required; but this is not the place to enter fully into details of the actual technique, and it must be taken for granted that the reader has some familiarity with the principles of the craft or can read it up in one of the many books on the subject.

Various fibres are used in African weaving. In the West Coast and the Congo finely split unspun raffia is very common, screw-pine is also said to be used in parts of Nigeria. Cotton is common on the West Coast and also silk, while a mixture of silk and cotton is used in some pattern weaving in Nigeria, and raffia and cotton in Dahomey. These variations in material add to the interest of the textures of the cloths produced.

Choice of colour is, or was before the introduction of synthetic dyes, dependent on the material used. Raffia was dyed with vegetable dye and most commonly patterned in black or red on a natural ground, but within the colour range could be found all shades of red and yellow ochres, siennas and sepias, greys, lavender-pinks and faded yellows. Cotton in Nigeria is dyed with local indigo, giving a range of blues, but imported dyes are also used. Ghana silk weaving is often a mass of brilliant colour, and it is said that the first imported silk cloth from Europe was unpicked and rewoven by Ashanti weavers in order to incorporate the bright new colours in their own designs.

The types of pattern which can be made in weaving can roughly be divided into two groups. First come those which are produced in a piece of plain weaving simply by the arrangement of different coloured threads in the warp or weft, or both. Coloured threads in the warp will result in longitudinal stripes of which the number, width and colour are arbitrary; while, when they are used in the weft, transverse stripes will be produced across the width of the material. If both transverse and longitudinal stripes

countries; drawn out of the writings of the Portuguese Duante Lopez, in Rome. 1591. Newly translated from the Italian and edited by Margareta Hutchinson. London, 1891.
[1] Ling Roth, *Studies in Primitive Looms*. 3rd edition. Halifax, 1950.

RAFFIA PILE CLOTH

Bushongo Tribe   *Belgian Congo*

TEXTILE DESIGN

are introduced the resulting pattern may be in the form of a check. A great variety of striped and checked pattern may be obtained in this way. If, for instance, red, green and white are used in both warp and weft, combinations of red crossed with red, or green, or white, and green crossed with green or white, and white crossed with white will give six variations in colour. If there are more warp than weft threads to an inch the weft will be largely hidden and the weave is called warp faced; if the position is reversed and the warp hidden by the greater number of weft threads it is known as tapestry weave. Then the width of the different bands of colour may be varied, and a further interest added by the use of threads of varying thicknesses, or even of differing fibres. Plate XVa gives some indication of such simple pattern.

More complicated forms of pattern weaving are introduced by allowing certain threads to pass over one or more than one thread in either warp or weft. To do this the warp threads are sometimes set up in pairs together, and only the ones needed for the pattern are used, the others are floated at the back until needed. Alternatively a double weft is used, and the coloured one forming the pattern is floated on the right side of the material directly above the plain coloured one which is woven in to form the ground. It will be woven right across the cloth, or worked backwards and forwards over certain small areas as the pattern requires. The pattern is then practically invisible on the wrong side. In the Congo patterned weaving is often carried out in natural coloured raffia only, forming what is known as diaper, or plain coloured pattern.

By these technical means an unlimited number of patterns can be woven, and infinite variations on simple geometrical designs are found in African cloths, although superficially they conform remarkably to type. The motifs are most often geometrical, but will range from broad stripes to delicate diagonal and zigzag lines; other favourite forms are solid triangles and lozenge shapes; while in some cloths more or less stylized human or animal forms can be found. A very characteristic arrangement in African textile design, on either woven or printed cloth, is the division of the material into bands or panels which are each filled with repetitions of one particular motif. These bands or panels are sometimes separated from each other by borders of stripes or plain uncoloured weaving.

EMBROIDERED CLOTH
(Plates XIX, XX, XXI, XXII, XXIII)

Both barkcloth and woven textiles may be further decorated with various forms of embroidery. It is not always easy to gather from the writings of the early explorers just

29

what was found in Nigeria when they first arrived, although several accounts would suggest embroidered as well as woven material. It would be interesting to see, for instance, the hangings in the royal buildings at Benin. Fawckner (1825) tells of 'a large hall hung with the most superb cloths of the country like tapestry'. Burton (1862) talks of seeing in the same place 'Fine cotton work, open and decorated with red worsted'. And Punch (1890) describes 'pieces perhaps six feet long or more, with life sized figures worked with a needle on the open-worked cotton material'.[1]

The most famous, and certainly the most beautiful, African embroidery comes from the area around the confluence of the Sankuru and Kasai rivers in the Congo, where it was carried out by the various sub-tribes of the Bushongo or Bakuba. The work is of such a high quality both in design and in technical achievement that it deserves special consideration here. It is said by Torday and Joyce[2] that the craft cannot be traced further back than the early seventeenth century among the Bushongo, and that the Mbala tradition was that Shamba Bulongongo, the most famous king of the Bushongo, learnt the art from the Pende and brought it back to his own country. Today it is considered that the origin of the craft may well have been the Lower Congo.

The embroidery was worked on a loosely woven, coarse-stranded raffia cloth which was first pounded in water or worked with the hands until it was as soft and supple as possible. This canvas was sometimes left the natural colour or sometimes dyed red with *Takula* (*Pterocarpus*) or blue with indigo. All shades of blue-purple, Indian red, or lavender pink can be found. Both ground and embroidery together were sometimes left a natural colour, or both dyed red after the work was completed.

The embroidery fibres were dyed red, yellow, mauve or black, or various shades of brown, or whitened with some mineral substance, or left the natural colour. With only simple vegetable dyes available the colour range was limited, but there were many fine gradations and the effect was subtle and beautiful. The raffia for the embroidery strands was split as finely as possible and worked in the hands until it was very soft; several threads were then twisted together and threaded through an iron needle.

The best known of these embroideries are the pile cloths (Plate XIX). In this type of work the shapes were filled in by threading the needle under one strand of the weave and pulling the fibre through until only about 2mm. were left on the far side of the stitch. The fibre was then cut off at the same height on the near side, and when this stitching had been repeated closely over the whole area, the result was a smooth,

---

[1] Quoted. Ling Roth, *Great Benin*, p. 141.

[2] Torday and Joyce, 'Notes ethnographiques sur les peuples communément appéles Bakuba'. *Annales du Musée du Congo Belge*. Series III. Tome II. Fasc. I. Brussels, 1910, pp. 183 et seq.

Further reference. Torday, *On the trail of the Bushongo*. London, 1925.

unknotted, brushlike surface resembling a pile velvet. The work was so finely done that the embroidery fibres did not appear on the wrong side. Various different ways of outlining or filling the motifs were employed, giving interesting changes of texture. Sometimes the forms were outlined in black stem stitch, sometimes several rows of stem stitching in different colours surrounded the central filling. Sometimes the filling was not continuous, the pile being worked as separate dots without continuity, sometimes it was cut very short, sometimes longer, and sometimes not cut at all, being left in loops.

To the west of the Bushongo area, particularly among the Mbala, more ordinary forms of embroidery were worked as well as the pile cloths (Plates XX, XXI). The stitch used was either stem stitch or a complicated form of chain stitch, while in some of the early eighteenth century Mbala cloths a type of drawn thread work was also done. The raffia canvas used for this work was of a very fine quality and the embroidery most delicate. Sometimes the ground was dyed black and the designs embroidered in natural tones upon it, sometimes the whole work was dyed red when finished. The pattern motifs used by the Bushongo are discussed in a separate section. Embroidery was always a woman's craft.

Other embroideries to which reference must be made are those of the Hausa, Fulani, and other peoples of Northern Nigeria. Here robes and curiously shaped wide trousers are covered with the most elaborate pattern work in coloured and gold and silver thread. Plate XXIIa shows a part of a beautiful scarlet robe embroidered with silver and gold from Bida in Northern Nigeria; the detail is very finely done, and the total effect of the robe, with the front panels and the back of the shoulders embroidered, is extraordinarily rich. The embroidered robes in Plate XXIII are of a rather different type, being far less elaborately covered than those illustrated above. The decoration of the portion of the wide trousers illustrated in b consists of a number of motifs put together in a somewhat haphazard way, very different from the regular balanced work of the previous examples.

PATCHWORK

Patchwork is not a common method of decoration in Africa, and the few pieces which can be found in the museums are old cloths worn by the Bushongo women at certain ceremonies.[1] They are made from a number of small triangular, rhomboid, or rectangular pieces of barkcloth, some dark brown or black, others a light natural

[1] Torday and Joyce, ibid. p. 180.

colour sewn together with fibre. There is nothing very striking about them, but it is interesting to note that this method of pattern making with textiles was indigenous in Africa.

APPLIQUÉ
(*Plates XXIV, XXV*)

Appliqué, or the ornamentation of cloth by stitching on either pieces of fabric of another colour, or completely different material such as beads, cowrie shells, metal plates, and so on, is found among the West Coast tribes; and also, albeit in a very different style, among the Bushongo of the Congo. In the great kingdoms of the West Coast its use seems to have been restricted to ceremonial functions or associated with civil or military power. Talbot[1] talks of 'the old war banners of the Kalabari tribes' being of appliqué work, while many of the symbols associated with the kingship and queen-mothership of the Ashanti collected by Meyerowitz[2] are from appliqué cloths, but most information about the use and technique of such cloths is given by Herskovits[3] in his account of the Dahomey.

These cloths were made by members of an especially restricted family guild for the use of those of rank and power. The craftsmen lived in a compound near the royal palace, and no such work was done anywhere in the country save by the men of this group only. We have accounts of the work from comparatively early days of British exploration, for Forbes describes it in 1849 and Skertchly in 1874.

Appliqué work was used for such things as state umbrellas, chiefs' caps, banners of associations, distinguishing marks of companies in the army and other groups; and for pavilions, hammocks, and hangings in chiefs' houses. The motifs were heraldic devices or symbols, or the insignia of kings; and the achievements of great men or incidents from everyday life were recorded in pictorial form. Herskovits believes that the designs used were derived from the bas-reliefs which decorated the walls of the royal palaces, and while there may have been no formal copying of actual reliefs the similarity of subject matter and the necessity in both techniques for large simple treatment of forms would lead to certain resemblances. The greater number of motifs were those of animals which were the symbolic forms used to set forth the greatness of the king and the royal dynasty.

[1] Talbot, *Tribes of the Niger Delta*. London, 1932, pp. 276, 335.
[2] Meyerowitz, *The Sacred State of the Akan*. London, 1951. Chap. VI.
[3] Herskovits, *Dahomey*. Vol. II, pp. 329 et seq.

According to Meyerowitz[1] the craft was first learnt in Dahomey from a Brazilian Portuguese who had settled in Widah. It is said that the work was originally done on raffia cloth, but that European trade cloth had been used since 1890. The background was usually a brilliant gold or black, figures were done in red or black; while purple, blues or greens were the predominating auxiliary colours. Patterns of individual figures, traditionally stylized, were kept for regular use, but motifs and forms altered from generation to generation of workers in the craft. Technically appliqué necessitates the main motifs in the design being worked in bold silhouette, with details such as features and the texture of hair, scales or feathers, or the patterning of clothing, indicated in a conventional manner by stitchery.

PAINTED CLOTH
(Plates XXVI, XXVII)

The weaving of patterns, or the decoration of plain cloth by covering it with embroidery, or by sewing on pieces of other material of differing colour and texture does not by any means exhaust the possibilities of textile design, for another vast field is opened up through the use of paint and dye.

Obviously the first form of painted decoration on cloth was made by the straightforward method of applying the paint with a finger or some simple kind of brush; making a pictograph to tell a story, or marking the cloth with a symbol or identification sign, or ornamenting it with a pattern. Decorated cloths of this kind can be found in many parts of Africa, the work being done on both woven fabric and barkcloth. It is often crude and clumsy and lacking in any real sense of design, but some cloths from the Congo painted in this way in greys, blacks and browns on a light ground are very beautiful. Indeed the almost complete freedom from any technical considerations in this kind of work makes for most spontaneous and lively results.

In India a highly skilled technique of outlining a design on the fabric with a reed pen and painting in the colours by hand was developed. It is interesting to note that a very similar method was used in Ghana. In the British Museum are two specimens of painted decoration on imported white cotton drill. The outlines of the pattern appear to have been drawn with a pen in brownish-black and certain areas are closely filled with scroll-like linework resembling Arabic characters in the same colour. Other smaller areas are solidly painted in green, red or yellow. The work has none of the finish or delicacy of Indian textile design, but it is even more remote from the simple broad

[1] Communication.

irregular treatment of other specimens of African painted pattern illustrated here. It has much in common with the fine embroidery on the robes of Moslems in the northern territories of the West Coast, and would appear to be an attempt at imitating this work in a cheap and rapid fashion.

PRINTED CLOTH
(*Plate XXVIII*)

In the decoration of textiles the desire for the regular repetition of the pattern unit over a large area calls for some mechanical method of reproduction which will be quicker and more precise than free painting. Some tribes cut stencil plates from the thick green sheaths of the stem of the plantain, or print with simple units cut on a cross section of a stick. But the finest examples of African skill in printing on cloth are the *Adinkira* stamp-printed cloths made by the Ashanti. The stamps used are cut from small pieces of calabash, and a very large number of different motifs are used. Rattray[1] gives drawings of some fifty of them, with the names by which they are known. As even in a large calabash the curve of the skin is perceptible it is not possible to cut a piece sufficiently flat for a stamp larger than three inches in diameter, while most stamps are considerably smaller. Several long slivers of bamboo are stuck into the back of the stamp and tied together a few inches from the base, forming a handle. The motifs are sometimes cut right through the thin calabash skin, or sometimes left in low relief. The cloth used is of woven cotton, sometimes left white, sometimes dyed russet brown with the bark of a tree. The black dye used for printing is prepared from another kind of bark which is cut up and boiled for several hours together with lumps of iron slag. After two thirds of the water has evaporated the remainder is strained off and the dye which is left is of the colour and consistency of coal tar. The cloth is pegged out with small wooden pins on a piece of flat ground for printing and the stamp then dipped in the dye and pressed on to the cloth.

In the type of stamp printing described above, the stamps have been designed as separate units each complete in itself, and are usually so used; they do not normally form part of a continuous flowing pattern as do blocks used for printing in both Europe and the East. Arab influence along the East Coast of Africa brought this different approach to the craft and at Zanzibar wood blocks were being used by the Swahili for printing *kangas* in the early part of this century which could be repeated to form a continuous pattern with no signs of a join. Some of these blocks were cut in

[1] Rattray, *Religion and Art in Ashanti*. Oxford, 1927. Chap. XXV.

low relief, others had groups of wooden pins stuck into the face of the block by which spots were printed. Many of the actual motifs used, as well as this difference in technique, betray the Eastern origin of the craft in this part of Africa.

Dyed Cloth, Tie Dyeing
(Plate XXIX)

Pattern printing with a stick, stamp, or block produces a darker motif on a light ground, other processes achieve the opposite effect by so treating the pattern areas that, when the whole cloth is immersed in the dye bath, they are left light while the rest of the fabric takes up the colour. There are two main methods of doing this; one, known as tie dyeing, consists in tying or sewing certain parts of the cloth so tightly together that the dye is unable to penetrate them; the other in covering the pattern units with either a wax or a paste, so that the dye cannot sink in. This is called the Resist method or Batik. Both crafts are practised in Africa, chiefly in Nigeria.[1]

An examination of specimens of African tie dyeing shows several variations in technique which produce different effects. A narrowly woven strip of cloth may be gathered horizontally at intervals and the gathering fibre drawn tight, after which raffia is bound tightly round the gathered portions so that the prepared material resembles a rope. When opened out after dyeing the cloth shows a series of horizontal undyed lines, varying according to the closeness of the gathering and the thickness of the material. When the cloth is caught up into little peaks bound tightly with raffia the result after dyeing is a white spot on the dyed cloth. A skilled craftsman can so twist his protecting fibre that the spot becomes a square or an oblong. If the cloth is bound round with parallel bands of fibre below the peak a number of concentric rings of light will result. Seeds or small stones can also be tied into the cloth to produce a spotted effect. Although the shapes which can be produced by this process are rather restricted, consisting simply of dots, circles, and parallel or zigzag lines running in one direction only; or, through the gathering of many little bunches of stuff close together, a splashed effect; yet very attractive cloths can be produced by the grouping of the pattern forms.

A modification of the tying technique is obtained by stitching the cloth. A pattern is sometimes carefully embroidered on a cloth with finely stranded raffia, and after dyeing the stitching is completely unpicked leaving the light ground showing. A chequered texture can be produced by darning the cloth with fibre, and animal or other forms are sometimes picked out in this way. The Jukun of Nigeria outline a design

[1] 'Art in the Drying Field'. *Nigeria* 30. 1949, pp. 325 et seq.

on the cloth by stitching strips of palm fibre along it before dyeing,[1] while the Bushongo of the Congo sew small pieces of reed or cane over the parts of the cloth which they wish to protect from the dye.[2] The Yoruba and the Tiv of Nigeria make many tie-dyed cloths, using the local indigo for their dye.[3, 4]

The Musée de l'Homme possesses one or two very interesting pieces of tie dyeing from the Ivory Coast. The material used is very finely woven raffia cloth which would appear to have been tied and dyed twice, the colours being the natural light yellow ochre, a darker red ochre, and black. The interest of the specimens lies in the fact that after dyeing the cloth has been deliberately left puckered and crimped instead of being stretched out and flattened, so that it has a curious spongy elastic texture.

Nigerian craftsmen are aware of the beauty which small irregularities of texture or colour can give to a work, for it is said of the tie dyeing method that sometimes red cotton is used for the sewing; this stains the cloth and, although it will later wash out, gives a finish which may help to sell it, just as does the indigo which is often applied superficially to cloth at the end of the dyeing process in order to give a temporary sheen which is valued by the buyers.

DYED CLOTH, RESIST METHOD
(*Plate XXX*)

The methods of sewing reeds on to the cloth or embroidering it with cotton or other fibre threads leads on to resist printing. In true resist printing the parts of the cloth which are not required to take the dye are covered either with wax or with a starch paste which will resist the penetration of the dye stuff into the material.

Amongst the Yoruba two different methods are practised. In one starch paste is painted on to the material directly with a feather or other tool. In the second a zinc-foil stencil is cut, clearing away the parts which are to be left white on the cloth. The stencil is then placed over the fabric and the paste painted through it with a piece of wood. Tin or even leather is also used for a stencil plate. After the paste has been put on to the cloth by either method it is dried until hard. The cloth is then dyed and after drying the surface paste is flaked off and the remainder finally boiled out.

[1] Meek, *Northern Nigeria*. Vol. I, p. 163.

[2] Torday and Joyce, 'Notes ethnographiques sur les peuples communément appelés Bakuba, ainsi que sur les peuplades apparentés les Bushongo'. *Annales du Musée du Congo Belge*. Series III. Tome II. Fasc. I. Brussels, 1910.

[3] Mrs. Daniels, 'Yoruba Pattern Dyeing'. *Nigeria* 14. 1938, pp. 125 et seq.

[4] K. C. Murray, 'Tiv Pattern Dyeing'. *Nigeria* 32. 1949, pp. 41 et seq.

It is said that there is no evidence that stencilled resist pattern making among the Yoruba has been introduced by Europeans, but it is a craft which is still developing and the motifs used are not necessarily traditional but are sometimes representations of men, animals and objects. Older pieces of resist printing which have been collected are usually strictly geometrical in their patterning, although some have simple stylized representational forms. Imported cotton goods from Manchester striped in bright reds, yellows and other colours, and also floral chintzes, were often over-printed locally in indigo by both the resist and tie dyeing methods so that in the lighter portions protected from the final dyeing, the original colours and patterns were left exposed. This often gave a very interesting effect to the cloths.

By the use of the stencil the treatment must in some ways be more limited than in freely painted work, because as in all stencilling, the solid portions of the plate must remain tied together, thus breaking the pattern units. One specimen in the British Museum has a fish scale pattern with a number of concentric curves on each scale: the cloth may have been covered with paste and the pattern then combed off.[1]

Dyed Cloth, the Discharge Method
(Plates XXXI, XXXII)

In this method of pattern printing the whole material must first be dyed. The design is then produced by printing or painting on the prepared background with a powerful reducing agent which removes the colour and so leaves a white or pale coloured pattern on a darker ground. The technique was not used in Europe until the beginning of the nineteenth century, and would seem to require considerable scientific or empirical knowledge.

A collection of cotton cloths printed by the people of Mali and particularly the Bambara was brought to the Musée de l'Homme by the late Fr. de Zeltner in the early part of this century. In his description[2] of the technique used he clearly describes a discharge method, resulting in white designs on fairly dark ground. The woman who dyed the material first prepared a dye bath by boiling the bark or leaves of certain trees for three hours. The cloth was immersed in the brownish liquid for about a day and then rinsed. Then, using a piece of iron as a tool, the design was painted on in a special mud, probably containing iron acetate, which was found at

[1] See Mrs. Daniels, 'Yoruba Pattern Dyeing'. *Nigeria* 14, pp. 125 et seq.; 'Art in the Drying Field'. *Nigeria* 30, pp. 325 et seq; Wenger and Beier, 'Adire, Yoruba pattern dyeing'. *Nigeria* 54. 1957.
[2] Clouzot, *Tissus Nègres*. Paris.

the bottom of certain pools. When dry the pattern was gone over again with locally made soap on the iron tool. This soap was obtained by soaking ashes in certain vegetable oils and it contained a good deal of potash which acted as a mordant. The pattern was then covered once more with mud and dried in the sun. Finally the cloth was beaten with a rod, rubbed between the hands, and rinsed in water to remove all traces of mud, and the pattern stood out white on the dark ground.

The patterns which can be produced by both the resist and discharge methods are somewhat similar, as both allow for free drawing on the cloth. As may be seen from the illustrations, very fine clear-cut detail has been obtained in the Bambara discharged cloths, although from the description of the covering of the patterned portions first with mud, then soap, and then mud again, it would seem extraordinarily difficult to avoid thick, blurred lines.

A study of a number of these cloths from slightly different areas shows interesting differences and similarities in motifs. Some rely entirely on the effect of linear patterns, others use more solid areas set against portions broken with fine line. Certain motifs can be found repeated on more than one cloth. The general effect of the cloths is of a more disciplined type of pattern than that found on the resist printed cloths of Nigeria; and considering the great technical skill required to get clear-cut lines in work of this type they reach a very high standard indeed.

CHAPTER V

Ornamental Basketry

It would be impossible fully to cover the infinite variety of pattern which can be found in African, or any other, basketwork. The very techniques of the craft themselves with all their variations produce a large number of patterns in texture over the surface of the baskets, and these may be further exploited through the development of the possibilities of each type of weave by the introduction of variations in materials and colour.

WOVEN BASKETRY
(Plates XXXIII, XXXIV, XXXV, XXXVI, XXXVII)

The type of pattern motif which is possible in woven basketry is similar to that found in the related techniques of cloth weaving and matting. Although in a large number of cases the pattern is woven in the body of the basket itself, it is obviously impossible to produce delicate and detailed patternwork with the tough and comparatively thick fibres and splints which are necessary for strength of construction. For this reason the finest examples of woven pattern are found almost without exception in small baskets which are first constructed of bark or of woven fibres and reeds of the required toughness and then covered with a very finely woven decorative outer case. In this way most beautiful specimens are made both in the lower Congo and in parts of Rhodesia.

In some techniques baskets are plaited rather than woven in a similar manner to the plaiting of strips for mat making.

39

ORNAMENTAL BASKETRY

COILED BASKETRY
(Plates XXXIII, XXXV, XXXVI)

In some parts of Africa coiled basketry is more common than woven. In this technique a central core of grass or reed is sewn with fibre thread in a flat or ascending spiral. The core itself is usually invisible, though not always so, and the pattern is produced through the colouring of the stitching. Often the colour scheme is restricted to black or brown or red with the natural coloured fibre; or, as in the case of baskets and trays made by the Nubian and Swahili women of East Africa, the work is a mass of brilliant colour produced by imported synthetic dyes. In this form of work equally interesting pattern can be produced on a large as on a small scale.

BASKETS SHOWING VARIATIONS IN MATERIALS OR TEXTURE
(Plates XXXVI, XXXVII)

Finally a random search through the basketry from Africa in any large museum collection will reveal a number of baskets in which the decorative interest lies either in the combination of several different techniques, or in the use of two or more very different types of fibre, or the combination of woven basketry with some entirely different material such as wood. This emphasizes the African's great love of texture as apart from colour or form, which becomes obvious in the study of his craftsmanship in any material.

CHAPTER VI

Beadwork

(Plates XXXVIII, XXXIX)

Apart from the use of beads in the making of head, neck and facial ornaments they are largely used in West, East and South Africa for the making of patterned covers for all kinds of things such as pots, calabashes of all sizes, drums, staves, fetish objects, masks and the like. They are also sewn on to cloth to decorate belts, boots, bags, robes, and other articles of apparel.

In both West and East Africa beadwork is especially associated with the decoration of chiefs' robes and crowns; or with the covering of objects connected with royal regalia or of other things held sacred in the same way. As would be expected, much of the design has a symbolic significance, and complete appreciation of it would depend upon knowledge and understanding of local tradition and symbolism. Superficially the technique lends itself best to the making of geometrical motifs such as triangles, zigzags, and interlacing pattern. Trade beads are usually employed, the resulting colours being bright and strong. These are sometimes arranged with real appreciation; but often, especially in modern work, are no more than a dull combination of dark blue, red and white.

CHAPTER VII

The Decoration of Hides and Leather

Skins, both in the form of raw hide among primitive peoples, and dressed leather among the more technically advanced, have always been very widely employed. Not only can they be used for clothing, but also to make screens and shelters, harness and binding thongs, shields and scabbards, shoes, sandals, bags, water pots, and containers of all shapes and sizes. It is therefore not surprising to find that a number of different methods have been evolved for their decoration.

SHAVEN PATTERN
(*Plate XL*)

In East Africa some tribes decorate skins from which the hair has not been removed, by shaving it off in certain parts; they may either clear small solid areas in this way, or form the pattern with narrow shaven lines.

PATTERN CARVED IN LOW RELIEF
(*Plate XL*)

Thick, tough hide can be carved in low relief in very much the same way as wood or calabash, and this treatment is sometimes used to ornament sheaths and scabbards. If a dark hide is used, and the cleared portions of the pattern are rubbed with a white chalky material, they will stand out clearly.

42

THE DECORATION OF HIDES AND LEATHER

In fine leather work parts of the surface leather may be excised to form small checkered designs.

APPLIQUÉ WORK ON RAW HIDE
(*Plate XL*)

A yet more ornate method of decorating raw hide was that carried out on the fans used in Benin. To quote C. Punch[1] (1889) 'It was always "quite the thing" for an African potentate to have at least two slaves fanning him. The usual shape of Bini fans was . . . (as illustrated). They were made of cowhide (green) with the hair on, and bright coloured pieces of flannel or Hausa leather were sewn on to make the pattern. No Ukoba, starting out to make himself a nuisance to some village, would feel quite dressed without one of these fans—in fact, except for the anklet and necklet, the fan was all he took in the way of clothes.' Elsewhere we have reports of these fans, the dark hairy skin decorated with scarlet flannel appliqué, sewn in place with strips of thin yellow skin. Various motifs, including stylized human and animal forms, seem to have been used in their making.

PAINTED HIDE SHIELDS
(*Plate XLI*)

Perhaps the most exciting patterns on hides are the painted designs on shields, used by certain tribes in East Africa. The shields are painted in earth colours, usually red, black and white, and are most striking. The patterning of the two halves of the shield is more often than not asymmetrical, but is always well balanced and arranged with due regard to its basic shape. Amongst the Masai and kindred tribes a form of heraldry has been developed by which those who know the signs can tell the district from which the warrior has come, and whether he is considered by his fellows to be a brave man, and so on.[2]

---

[1] Quoted. Ling Roth, *Great Benin*, p. 123.
[2] See Hobley, *The Ethnology of the Akamba*. Cambridge, 1910, p. 127.

THE DECORATION OF HIDES AND LEATHER

DECORATION OF TANNED LEATHER
(Plates XLII, XLIII)

Turning to decorative work in tanned leather we find it to be the main traditional export of the peoples of Northern Nigeria as well as being extensively used in their own daily life.[1] In a description by Dodwell[2] of the leather work at Oyo in Nigeria it is stated that the skins used are almost exclusively goat skins; in the past sheep or various game skins were also used but never those of horses or cattle. Although imported dyes are now sometimes used the traditional ones are locally made. These consist of black from a mixture of pieces of old iron, starch, and ashes from the blacksmiths' workshops; red from the outer strippings of the bulrush millet together with salt and wood ash; yellow from a paste of ginger and lime juice; blue from indigo. For green and white the leather had to be untanned, when green was made from a mixture of copper filings, lime and copper sulphate; and white by rubbing in palm oil. A very similar list is given from Kano by Hambly.[3]

The most simple form of decoration in Northern Nigeria is said to be done by drawing arabesques on the leather with black ink, but patchwork and appliqué in which motifs in contrasting colours are first gummed and then sewn to the basic skin with narrow thongs are better known. The applied patches are further decorated with coloured stitching. In some cases checkered designs are made by the excision of parts of the surface leather.

The design motifs are traditional, and similar to those used in local embroideries with very few variations. As in most Moslem art they are largely geometrical, but stylized men, animals, birds and reptiles are also to be found as can be seen from the illustration of the cover from Bida (Plate XLIII).

Very similar work in leather can be found further south; it does not always have the same standard of technical perfection as work from the north, but may compensate by more original and interesting design.

[1] Jeffries, 'Leatherwork in Northern Nigeria'. *Nigeria* 14. 1938.
[2] Dodwell, 'The Tim-tim makers of Oyo'. *Nigeria* 42. 1953.
[3] Hambly, *Culture areas of Nigeria*. Chicago, 1935.

CHAPTER VIII

Cicatrization and Body Painting

(*Plates XLIV, XLV*)

A study of African pattern would not be complete without mention of the practice of cicatrization, and also of the painting of designs on the face and body with the juice of certain plants or with ochre or chalk. Such customs are dying out, but can still be found amongst the more unsophisticated people.

It is, after all, common to the human race and to women especially, to attempt to enhance natural beauty by some form of decoration. Amongst many people this is confined to costume or hair styles, or to painting such prominent parts as the face or finger nails, but the African carries the art considerably further. Living in a hot climate he has more exposed parts of his body to decorate, and he does this with the thoroughness with which he would decorate a calabash or any other vessel.

The African prizes an oiled and polished body, although sometimes he produces a matt surface by smearing it with clay or colouring matter. Both oiling and covering the body with colour are usually done for the dance. The hair is often trimmed and plaited into various styles, and certain teeth may be extracted or filed to a point.

In Nigeria some tribes ornament their faces and bodies with the most delicate and intricate patterns painted with vegetable juice, but the most usual form of decoration is cicatrization. There are several reasons for the practice; it is a common custom among a very large number of tribes to mark their members with the tribal mark, very often on the temples; then medicine, both curative and preventive, also employs this device, when the body may be cut and rubbed with medicine supposed to contain magical properties; but the most highly developed schemes of decoration are made for aesthetic purposes, to give visual and tactile pleasure to young people in their more intimate personal relationships. Not every tribe which practises cicatrization carries the art to a high standard, often the work consists merely of a few rows of parallel scars, but, as may be seen from the illustrations, many highly elaborate and beautiful patterns may be found, especially among the tribes in the centre of the Congo. Here the most ornate designs are to be found covering the whole body.

'Il faut souffrir pour être belle', and the descriptions which are given of all forms of cicatrization seem painful and unpleasant. Both abstract designs and stylized forms are cut on all parts of the body—forehead, temples, cheeks, neck, legs and arms, chest, stomach, buttocks, thighs and legs; the marks are usually made by cutting the skin with a sharp knife or razor, and then rubbing charcoal or vegetable matter into the wounds so that they finally heal as raised, shiny keloids.

Bohannan[1] writes that there are changing fashions, both in motif and techniques, in Tiv cicatrization; and the decorations are used to emphasize the natural good points of the wearer's face or body. By using a technique which will make deep scarifications, for instance, prominent cheeks may be made more prominent; and the apparent shape of a nose can be altered at will. A good pair of legs, too, will attract more notice if tastefully decorated with a large and outstanding band of pattern. The Tiv take a great deal of trouble in trying out various patterns to see which fit their faces best. The young ones do this by painting with the juice of a certain plant, while a more lasting trial run may be taken by pricking the face with the twig of a tree which leaves a round white scar for two or three months. The actual process of cicatrization, with the list of patterns used in Dahomey with their names and sites on the body, has been given by Herskovits.[2]

---

[1] Bohannan, 'Beauty and Scarification among the Tiv'. *Man.* Vol. LVI, 1956, 129.
[2] Herskovits, *Dahomey.* Vol. I, pp. 291 et seq.

CHAPTER IX

Calabash Patterns

The decoration of calabashes is one of the most interesting fields for the study of African pattern. Amongst the tribes which have a strong penchant for ornament the craft gives great opportunities, and a number of different techniques have been evolved, each giving its own interesting effects. From the written accounts available we can get a clear idea of some at least of these processes, and it is usually easy to pick out the various methods used from a systematic study of the collections of African calabashes in the museums. From the subject matter which is found in the designs we see clearly the pre-eminent position which allegory and symbolism hold in African design.

The preparation of a decorated gourd or calabash is a long and painstaking process. First the gourd must be prepared. For this it is taken when ripe and soaked in a stream or water hole until the contents are completely rotten. It is then opened, and the insides thoroughly cleaned out, after which it is dried in the sun. During the soaking the skin will have grown bloated and soft, but as it dries it becomes hard so that it can be worked like wood. By some tribes the calabash is cut into two horizontally, the top portion often being used as a lid for the base; while others cut it across vertically. The different shapes thus produced lead to very different forms of ornamentation.

The next consideration is the basic colour of the undecorated calabash, and here considerable variety may be produced. The natural colour is a warm yellow, and it is often left in this state. If the fine layer of the cuticle or outer skin is scraped off the craftsman has a white surface to decorate. Alternatively the calabash may be rubbed with a concoction of millet leaves which gives it a beautiful old rose colour, or it may be stained indigo, red, or deep orange or burnt sienna. After decoration these various

47

colours receive a further rich patina through constant handling and through hanging in a smoky hut until they show a sombre polish. So even with no decoration at all the basic colours and textures of calabashes cover a large range and some of them are very beautiful in themselves.

CARVED PATTERN
(*Plate XLVI*)

The techniques which are then used in calabash decoration fall into four main groups, although in actual practice the different methods are often combined. First comes a broad treatment in which either the background or the pattern motifs are cleared evenly to a depth slightly below the surface giving clear relief and colour change. If the calabash is intended for purely ornamental purposes the whole skin, which is not very thick, may even be cut away in places.

SCRAPED PATTERN
(*Plates XLVII, XLVIII, XLIX, L*)

Closely akin to this carving method comes that of scraping. Many variations of decoration are produced by outlining the pattern motifs with a sharp knife and then carefully scraping away the background area. Thus if the calabash is unstained the pattern will stand out yellow (the natural colour of the surface) on a white (scraped) ground. If the calabash has first been stained the design will be the colour of the stain used, on a ground which is either yellow (the stain alone having been rubbed off and the natural colour of the cuticle left unharmed) or white (if the cuticle is also removed). A reverse effect can be obtained, of course, by scraping away not the background, but the pattern motif itself.

SCORCHED PATTERN
(*Plates LI, LIId*)

A third method of decoration is done by lightly scorching the surface area of the pattern motifs with the flat surface of a knife or other tool, thus colouring them dark brown or black. When whole areas are thus treated another colour possibility is added.

48

CALABASH PATTERNS

Engraved Pattern
(Plates XLIX, L, LI, LII)

Finally come the engraving techniques. In these, large surfaces, either of the background or of pattern motifs, are covered with a texture of finely engraved line, very often cross hatched. These lines are sometimes incised with a sharp knife, sometimes burnt with a hot point. When the latter tool is used a texture of small burnt black dots instead of lines may be produced. The engraved pattern will show up white or black according to whether it has been cut or burnt against the natural coloured or stained parts of the calabash, and this contrast is sometimes accentuated by rubbing soot or chalk into the engraved lines. The technique may be used in such a way that the whole background or the whole surface of the pattern motifs are covered with a mass of texture pattern.

Decoration with Extraneous Materials
(Plate LIII)

The ornamentation of calabashes by the application of extraneous materials is known. In both South-east Africa and West Africa soft clay is pressed into incisions and coloured or white beads embedded in this base, either as ornamental motifs in themselves or used to outline bands of scorched pattern. Gourds are commonly completely encased in tightly fitting coverings of patterned beadwork, constructed round them but kept entirely separate. Patterns are sometimes 'embroidered' on calabashes, closely stitched with brass or steel wire or even, from the Ashanti in Ghana, with gold thread.

All these methods of carving, scraping, scorching or engraving pattern on calabashes are most suitable both for geometric design and for the representation in stylized form of animals, men, and other objects. When geometrical motifs alone are used, rich contrasts in texture may be obtained by leaving some forms in strong colour contrasted with others in white or buff. Some calabashes are further enhanced by the engraving of small texture patterns on certain areas. The calabash from Lagos (Plate XLVI) is a good example of bold, simple, geometrical treatment. It is interesting to compare it with the very fine specimen from the Foulbe of the Cameroons (Plate XLIXb) and to notice the added interest given to the latter through the use of finely engraved pattern in white line on the dark ground. In contrast to the angular type of motif which is so commonly found throughout Africa, the Tiv, Ibo and Ibibio of Eastern Nigeria decorate their calabashes with gracefully flowing curvilinear designs said to be

49

derived from the patterns painted on the skins of these people. The Hausa in Northern Nigeria use curves in their designs and curvilinear patterns are also scorched on the gourds of the Kiga in Western Uganda (Plate LI).

In West Africa, in territories such as Liberia and Nigeria and most probably a number of others, leaf forms are used in the decoration of calabashes and other objects. They may flow in a fairly naturalistic way over the surface of the object decorated, or they may be arranged in a rather unimaginative stylized pattern.

When we turn to the use of representational forms of men, animals and other objects in calabash decoration we find much that really shows no intention whatever of design. The figures are scattered about the body in a haphazard fashion and all that can be said for it from a designer's point of view is that the spaces are all filled. Without some sort of geometrical framework within which to set the motifs it is impossible to think of the rounded body of the calabash in terms of pattern, and the craftsmen were probably only concerned with recording a story or setting down a number of symbols for some specific purpose, they were not interested in the decorative appearance of the work in the least. But in the work of some tribes, notably those in Dahomey, bands of geometrical motifs such as bars, zigzags, triangles, checks and lozenges often divide other bands or panels which are filled with representational motifs and these designs are extraordinarily successful. The contrast between the different elements is satisfying as a start, while the actual design of the panels with their grotesque, slightly heraldic, stylized animals is excellent.

CARVED COCONUTS
(Plate LIII)

Some well-carved coconut shells from Benin may be found in the British Museum. We reproduce one here in order to show the very different technical treatment from that used in calabash decoration. The coconut shell is carved in low relief, the background being cut away and the raised portions of the motifs being finished with a slightly rounded surface. The technique resembles that of Nigerian wood carving and the work is far more naturalistic than most calabash design. This particular specimen is crudely cut and dates back to the end of the last century.

References:
Griaule et Dieterlen, 'Calebasses Dahoméennes', *Journal de la Société des Africanistes*. 1935. Tome. V. Fasc. II.
Hambly, *Culture Areas of Nigeria*. Chicago, 1935.

CALABASH PATTERNS

Murray, 'The Decoration of Calabashes by the Tiv'. *Nigeria* 36. 1951.
Herskovits, *Dahomey*. New York, 1938, Vol. II, pp. 344 et seq.
Lindblom, *The Akamba in British East Africa*. Uppsala, 1920.
Pitt Rivers, *Antique Works of Art from Benin*. 1900.

CHAPTER X

Decoration on Wood

TEXTURE PATTERN
(*Plates LIV, LV, LVI*)

The richness of surface texture shown in African carving is discussed in Chapter XIV. It is perhaps a more noticeable pattern element in wood carving than in work in any other material. But a general desire to cover the surface is by no means all that may be found in these carved patterns. In even the most simple there is usually some division between plain and decorated surfaces, the areas being broken up into bands or masses, and a conscious relationship between the pattern and the form of the object is nearly always shown. In Plate LV the central mass of the bodies of the two powder kegs has been fitly emphasized by the curving forms cutting across the surface pattern, while the stool from Mashonaland is a beautiful example of the relationship of pattern and form. Finally in the wooden vessel from the Kasai shown in Plate LVI we have a magnificent example of African pattern at its best. The flowing mass of the interlacing scrolls on the body, balanced by the well proportioned and skilfully carved bands of pattern covering the neck, combine to make a most impressive yet simple design.

REPRESENTATIONAL FORMS IN CARVED DESIGN
(*Plates LVII, LVIII, LIX*)

Wood, especially the hard woods, is a material which has a fair degree of permanence;

52

it is also one which can be worked to a high finish by a skilled craftsman and it allows considerable freedom in the carrying out of all kinds of design. It is, in fact, the best material available over the greater part of the area which we are studying, and so it is natural that a very large number of the objects used in the religious cults and in court ceremonial as well as in architectural features should be made of it. So, owing to the purposes for which these things are carved, another element enters into their decoration, the use of representational forms and of symbolism. One of the most beautiful pieces of African carving, illustrated here, is the wooden door decorated with fishes by the Baule tribe of the Ivory Coast, a people well known for their aesthetic sense. The fish are naturalistic, but have been placed in relationship to the shape of the panel with all the skill of a Chinese painting. Their broken textured surface catches the light and stands out in contrast to the ground with its slight suggestion of waves. The total effect of the work is most lovely. Door panels and mouldings offer great scope for carving, and the Yoruba of Nigeria take full advantage of it. The panels are often crowded with tiers of detailed carving depicting processions of chiefs or European officials on the march, or scenes which doubtless have some historic or traditional significance. They often show a nice sense of humour in their portrayal, not unlike the misericords and corbels in our medieval churches. In some, which are less crowded, a sense of pattern over-rides the subject matter; in all, the enjoyment of texture pattern creeps in, in the decoration of figures and trappings, or in the bands which divide one portion of the design from another. The moulding of a door frame from Zanzibar is illustrated here to contrast with Yoruba work. It cannot be called fully African, for it is the work of Swahili craftsmen in the Arab tradition. Yet as Arabic influence is strong in the coastal region of East Africa, it is interesting to note the very different characteristics of the flowing curves and plant forms which are used.

BLACK AND WHITE WOOD CARVING
(*Plates LX, LXIa, LXIIa*)

An effective technique which has been elaborated in East Africa and possibly in other parts also, is one which is very reminiscent of that used in calabash decoration. The object to be decorated is first stained black all over, and the pattern is then either engraved in white on the black ground, or left standing in black against the ground which has been cleared away to a depth of about one eighth of an inch and left white. Various types of ladles and vessels are found worked in this technique on the coast, while the Lacustrine Bantu tribes of Uganda and the Eastern Congo use it for arrow quivers, as well as for milk vessels and containers of different kinds.

PAINTED PATTERN ON WOOD
(Plate LXII)

Those tribes which use wooden shields in East Africa often decorate them as they would shields of hide, with painted pattern which almost certainly has a symbolic significance, in chalk and coloured earths; the resulting irregular geometrical design is most attractive. In a similar way pattern is painted on wooden objects such as masks, canoe prows, and vessels of various kinds in many parts of the continent.

SCORCHED PATTERN ON WOOD
(Plate LXIb)

Pattern is also found burnt on wood, in a technique which combines the scorching of large areas with the engraving of lines with a hot iron point. The Ibibio fans illustrated here are an example of this kind of work.

DECORATION OF WOOD WITH EXTRANEOUS MATERIAL
(Plate LXIII)

Finally there is the decoration of wood by the application of some foreign material. This takes many forms; sometimes strips of metal sheeting are applied, or beads or metal studs may be hammered into the wood. Perhaps one of the most interesting ways in which the technique was developed is that which was used by the Kamba of Kenya in the decoration of their stools. The old craftsmen first wound a fine spiral of brass or copper wire by twisting it closely round a piece of metal like a fine knitting needle. This was then slipped off and hammered horizontally into the surface of the wood which had previously been softened by soaking in oil.

CHAPTER XI

Ornamental Ivory Carving

(Plates LXIV, LXV)

In Africa the carving of ivory has been carried out in a very similar fashion to that of wood. It is, of course, usually done on a smaller scale, but the fact that, unlike wood, it may be carved without regard to its grain, allows for very fine detail in pattern work.

In the West Coast, and especially in Nigeria amongst the Yoruba and the Bini, various decorative objects were carved from sections of tusks; these included armlets, bowls, boxes and so on. They are carved in low relief, sometimes to a considerable depth, or, as in the case of the bracelet shown in Plate LXIVa, the work is carved in two separate layers interlocking as a Chinese puzzle does, with the design of the outer layer cut right through. In this example the inner layer is decorated with a pattern of finely drilled holes, and the small bird seen in the centre at the base is carved on the inner layer, being one of the points which prevent the two portions of the bracelet from coming apart. In this specimen and also in the Benin tusk in Plate LXVb the very great freedom of design which we also find in Yoruba wood carving is clearly to be seen, nevertheless it is well balanced and consistent in the planning of its masses. The bowl in Plate LXIVb is much more disciplined in its arrangement, as the figures are spaced at a regular distance round the sides. This piece is most interesting in the way in which the figure on the right has been freed from the normal frontal position without breaking the rhythm of the whole.

The two illustrations of the pitcher in Plate LXVc and d are most delightful. Here bands of interlacing pattern separate the panels on which animal motifs are carved.

55

In these we find many symbols and stylized animals which we associate with the work of Benin; the two-headed bird, the mud fish and the highly stylized head of an elephant seen from above, with a double trunk ending in hands holding leafed branches. Other representations such as the charming little antelope grazing on the branch of leaves are much more naturalistic.

The freely flowing pattern typical of the carving on Benin tusks has already been mentioned. The general effect of these carvings is very rich, but the more simplified treatment shown in the two tusks from Loango in the Lower Congo is more intelligible to the observer. In the first the figures are arranged in a spiral round the tusk, while in the second they are set in bands placed one above the other.

In many African ivory carvings, details such as the spots on animals, the eyes and tribal marking on human masks or faces, and stylized representations of hair, or suggestions of neck ornaments, are inlaid with strips or studs of iron, brass or copper.

CHAPTER XII

Decorative Metal Work

BEATEN METAL DESIGN
(*Plates LXVI, LXVII*)

There are two very different methods of decorating metal; one is by beating, the other by casting; of these the first is almost certainly the older. The term repoussé is often used for any kind of beaten metal work, but its correct definition is the raising of a pattern in relief by blows with a hammer and punches from the under side. A similar effect can be obtained by beating down the background from the front with the aid of punches. The term chasing is applied to the surface decoration of a piece of metal from the front. By producing an uneven texture in which parts of the surface are tilted to the light, or by using punches which themselves have a pattern element, many different textural qualities may be obtained, and this satisfies the African love of surface pattern. Herskovits[1] says that in Dahomey the most important part of the equipment of every brass worker was a set of iron dies which he made for himself. These were used to represent figures on cloth, patterns on animal pelts, hair, eyebrows and the like on human faces. From the context this would appear to refer to the *cire perdue* method of casting described below, but most authorities agree that there the decoration is done on the wax. Interesting variations in texture may be seen in the two brass medallions decorated by the repoussé method illustrated in Plate LXVI. In the Ashanti vessel shown in Plate LXVIIb the motifs are outlined with small holes punched into the brass and filled with white material. While beaten metal work is found in Ashanti, Dahomey and Southern Nigeria it is far more common further north, the chief centres being Bida and Kano.

[1] Herskovits, *Dahomey*. Vol. II, p. 356.

DECORATIVE METAL WORK
CAST METAL DESIGN
(Plates LXVII, LXVIII, LXIX)

Casting in West Africa is done by the *cire perdue* method. Briefly this technique consists in first making a rough model in clay of the object to be cast. This is then covered with a carefully modelled layer of beeswax in which every detail is exactly finished. The wax layer is constantly smoothed with a hot knife, and lines incised where necessary, while finely drawn threads of wax are attached to form raised lines. If the object to be cast is small it may be modelled completely in wax with no core, at other times a metal armature may be used. When the wax shell is completed and has hardened it is painted with successive coats of slurry (liquid clay) until the coating reaches a thickness of about $\frac{1}{8}$", and then encased in a thick clay mould. As the original wax model was made to include the sprue, or ducts and funnel through which the melted wax and steam could escape and the moulten metal enter, this apperture will also be formed in the fired clay mould. The moulten metal, heated in a clay crucible, is then run into the mould which is later broken up and the metal cast removed, and where necessary cleaned up. The technique of the casts made in Ashanti, Dahomy, and above all in Benin in the past was of a very high quality indeed and has given rise to much discussion as to its origin.

It is not easy to define the right qualities for design in metal casting as the work is not done directly on the material in which it will finally appear. The motifs have to be modelled or incised in soft wax which has very different qualities from the hard metal in which they will eventually be reproduced, so that the normal technical criteria of fitness for material and the appropriate tools for working in that material are missing. The motifs used in Benin bronze casting are discussed fully in the appropriate chapter; it is sufficient to notice here that both human and animal forms, or, on the other hand, purely geometrical design can be equally well carried out by the process, and where natural forms are used they may be very realistic or highly stylized. The curious combination of a comparatively small number of accepted stylizations within a representational formula in Benin casts is possibly partly a reflection of the lack of structural guidance in this technique.

CHAPTER XIII

Pottery Design

While in metal work, wood carving, cloth making and printing the African craftsman has developed very considerable skills, and exercises his ingenuity in working out methods of casting, constructing looms, printing and dyeing cloth and so on, yet with few exceptions his achievement in the craft of pottery has never reached an outstanding level. The preparation of clay is very perfunctory, nothing is known of an indigenous wheel beyond a simple turntable, no kiln is used for firing, and the use of a vitreous glaze is not attempted. Nor has the African aspired to build any great variety of shapes for his pottery, or to put it to many different uses. True, he has used pots for various magico-religious purposes from burial urns to pots containing poison or magic potions or sacrificial libations, but on the whole his chief need has been for cooking pots, water pots and beer pots, all vessels which will be subjected to rough and dirty treatment, and so unlikely to develop in him a desire to expend time and labour on the carrying out of delicate design.

So the soil of Africa from north to south and from east to west is littered with ill-fired sherds on which elementary pattern forms are scratched or impressed with roulettes of wood or of plaited reed, or by stamps made of natural objects such as corn cobs, shells and seeds. All these are interesting and even excellent examples of decoration by primitive methods, but one is struck by the lack of development and the difficulty of finding outstanding specimens which show a real feeling for design in the craft.

The most widespread methods of decorating pots found in Africa are those of impressing or stamping a pattern, or of engraving or incising one with a pointed stick or piece of iron; both these are carried out before firing when the pot is leather hard. Moulded decoration is also found, and in some areas pots are coloured or burnished.

IMPRESSED PATTERN
(*Plate LXX*)

Accounts of pot making and descriptions of pots and sherds from every part of the continent suggest an enormous variety of natural and manufactured objects used to impress simple patterns on the clay. Such decoration may spread all over the pot, or it may be formally arranged in zones often bounded by incised lines. The whole surface of the pot may be smoothed with a small stone placed in a damp cloth, when slight pressure in working will cause small circular indentations which satisfy the desire for interesting texture. This characteristic love of texture pattern which we notice in every African craft will find an equal pleasure in closely covering the surface with sharply cut indentations made with the finger nail. The sharp edge of a shell may be used to imprint a series of small holes or circles on the clay, or, to quote another description: 'Compressed chevrons are made by rocking and advancing a mussel shell held in the right hand. The shell is rocked on its rounded edge and moved simultaneously in a direction at right angles to the plane of that edge.' Parallel tracks may be hollowed out by drawing the tips of the fingers across the surface of the pot, and a series of little indentations by regular pressure with a piece of corn cob. The custom of plaiting little reed roulettes which are rolled round the neck or body of the pot to form bands of pattern is very common; these plaited roulettes will make a dotted diagonal or herring-bone pattern according to the way in which they are knotted (Plate LXXd). Many patterns are also made with roulettes carved from small pieces of wood, while some tribes impress a pattern with an iron ring. Our three illustrations of impressed pattern show first a large water pot from Uganda which is a fine specimen of a pot decorated with bands of roulette pattern. Then comes one which is indented, probably with a finger nail, over the whole surface of a clay face, but which is carefully arranged to emphasize the form. Notice the central dividing vertical line above the nose, with the curves following the eyebrows on either side, and the tall rectangular panels suggesting the cheeks. Finally pattern confined within definite bands. Such pattern is, practically without exception, rolled round the body of a pot in a series of concentric horizontal circles, and the specimen here shown is most unusual in the way in which the pattern element has been arranged on the body.

POTTERY DESIGN
Incised Pattern
(*Plate LXXI*)

Equally common, as a method of pot decoration, is the incising or engraving of a pattern with a knife, pointed stick, nail, shell, piece of wood or gourd with a serrated edge like a comb, or any other pointed object. The two styles of impressing and incising are often used together. Again this type of work is often crude and haphazard, but many well-shaped pots have bands of incised pattern emphasizing the changing silhouette, or are ornamented with geometrical shapes such as bands, triangles, lozenges, and so on, filled in with parallel lines or cross-hatching. These incised surfaces may be further emphasized by the filling-in of the engraved lines with white kaolin or crushed shell or taluka powder, or they may be arranged as matt surface forms surrounded by smooth areas burnished to a high gloss. Of this burnishing more will be said later.

Moulded Pattern
(*Plates LXXII, LXXIII, LXXIVa, b*)

A number of ceremonial bowls and terra cotta boxes may be found both on the West Coast and in the Congo which have human figures or animals modelled in high relief on the lids or body of the pot. Some of these fall rather into the class of small free-standing sculpture than that of decorative design. In Plate LXXIIb and c, are shown Ashanti pots in which the moulded element takes its place as part of the general design; while LXXIIa is a good example of the stylized treatment of figures in both Cameroon pottery and wood carving, when the arms and legs form a kind of lattice work round the body of the object.

Plate LXXIII shows various types of curvilinear moulded pattern, while Plate LXXIVa and b are two examples of patterns made by attaching pellets of clay to the body of the pot.

Coloured or Burnished Decoration
(*Plate LXXIVc, d*)

Next we come to the use of burnishing and the coating of pots with coloured vegetable or mineral matter. These processes may have either an aesthetic or a practical purpose; in some cases it is obvious that the desire to enhance or entirely conceal the dreary colour which is taken on by so much fired clay is the main reason for what is done; in others the practical advantage of rendering the vessel less porous is the chief motive. A very interesting account of colouring methods practised in the Congo is given in the *Annales du Musée du Congo Belge*.[1] The subject is divided into three sections; first the application of vegetable matter giving a matt surface, secondly of vegetable matter giving a glossy finish, and finally the use of mineral substances. For the first palm oil or other plant juices are applied after firing and are often put on as an even coating over the whole pot: in this case any variation in colour is fortuitous. At other times more purposeful decoration is obtained by painting or splashing on the colouring matter. In this way the people of the Lower and Middle Congo produce pottery with the appearance of marbling or the grain of wood; or, in other cases, the pot may look much like the map of an ocean filled with coloured islands and archipelagoes.

In some areas rudimentary decoration in the form of lines and geometrical motifs is painted on with the finger or a piece of stick, while in the Lower Congo Coast region motifs depicted in this way show signs of a zoomorphic origin.

Various gums and resins are used to give a glossy finish to the pots. Sometimes these are painted over the whole vessel, in others a more interesting effect is produced by leaving some areas with a matt surface, which, as has been said, is often filled in with an incised or impressed pattern.

Mineral matter, usually in the form of graphite, or of an iron ochre mixed with oil, is sometimes rubbed into a leather-hard pot and burnished before firing in many parts of Africa. As hard rubbing is required to produce a highly polished surface, no portion of the pot with incised or impressed pattern will stand up to the treatment; so that the decoration of the pot will consist in the arrangement of plain burnished masses contrasted with the decorated areas having a matt surface.

ENCASED POTS
(Plate LXXVIa, b)

An interesting little pot is shown in Plate LXXVIa. The neck and base are completely hidden in a woven fibre covering, which is continued as a handle. The body of the pot has a decorative binding of strips of cane, so that all that can be seen of the pot itself is a series of panels framed by the cane and decorated with roulette pattern. The planning of the total decorative effect, to include both the elements of the actual body

[1] 'Céramiques et Nattes'. *Annales du Musée du Congo Belge*. Series III. Tome II.

of the pot itself and also the extraneous casing, is notable. The second encased pot has an equally pleasing appearance, but in this example the entire surface of the pot is covered.

Cow Dung Bowls
(*Plate LXXVIc, d*)

Two other vessels are also illustrated, though neither, strictly speaking, comes into our geographical field of study, nor into a rigidly defined classification of pottery; but both should be of real interest to a student of African pottery design. These are a couple of bowls made of cow dung from the Nuba Hills in Kordofan. The pattern is painted in white and red earth, giving a rich and well designed effect which might well be adopted by the makers of pottery proper.

References:
Thomas, 'Pottery Making of the Ibo Speaking People', *Man.*, 1910, p. 53.
Schofield, *Primitive Pottery: An Introduction to South African Ceramics.* Handbook Series No. 3 of the South African Archaeological Society. Capetown, 1948.
Nicholson, 'Bida Pottery', *Man.*, 1929. 34.
Griaule et Lebeuf, 'Fouilles dans la région du Tchad'. *Journal de la Société des Africanistes.* Tome XVIII. Fasc. I.
Trowell, 'Some Royal Craftsmen of Buganda', *Uganda Journal.* Vol. VIII.

CHAPTER XIV

Motifs in African Design

lthough technological considerations play such an important part in defining the possibilities and limitations of decorative design that it has seemed best first to approach our subject from this angle, it is equally necessary and possibly more interesting to study the motifs used, regardless of the way in which they are worked out. So now, having thought through the implications of method, let us briefly examine the matter of African pattern.

It would seem obvious to divide it into three types; those of textural, representational and geometrical forms. At once we realize that there are no hard and fast boundaries to these groups, and that the one slides imperceptibly into the other; while all the time we are working along the edge of the impenetrable jungle of symbolism. Texture pattern, however, seems to be the most easy to define. Until comparatively recently any European study of design dealt only with specific pattern motifs; it might be classical ornament or floral pattern but, as such titles as 'The Anatomy of Pattern', 'The Grammar of Japanese Ornament and Design', or 'The Dictionary of Decorative Art' will show, decoration was conceived of as the ornamentation of an object with representational, even if stylized, forms; or at least with strictly geometrical designs. Students in schools of art studied natural forms, especially those of plants, they manipulated and twisted the plant as a whole, they dissected the flower and took cross sections of the seed capsules, and selected and re-grouped their results until they covered a surface with symmetrical clusters of flowers or fruits. It is only lately that our great interest in texture has developed. Perhaps it is due to our own preoccupation with its decorative possibilities that we notice the presence of texture pattern in African design; nevertheless, once we have noticed it, its predominance is most striking.

64

MOTIFS IN AFRICAN DESIGN

In making a study of any collection of African work we cannot fail to be struck by the extraordinary richness of surface texture which is conveyed through the use of small patterns over large areas. It is perhaps most noticeable in work on the harder materials, pottery, metal, wood, calabash and ivory, although it would seem highly probable that the attention of African craftsmen was drawn in the first place to the decorative interest of such pattern as it arose through the technical process of fibre weaving. For even the most simple weaves found in basketry, matting and woven textiles have satisfying textural effects; and a very slight variation in the order of work, or the substitution of another weight of fibre or a different colour in places, will alter the appearance of the whole thing. Such a simple form of ornamentation conveys no abstruse symbolic meaning, it is meant to be enjoyed for its own sake alone (Plates XVb, c, XIXc, XXXIIIc).

Similarly the handling of pottery before firing will give rise to natural forms of pattern; it may be slight irregularities of texture due to the pressure of the tool used in smoothing the vessel, or a groove caused accidentally by the finger tips, or a mottled effect obtained unintentionally when covering the pot with a coat of vegetable matter to render it less porous. It is often said that the idea of impressing a pattern on to the soft clay came from the custom of lining baskets with clay and then burning off the fibre covering in the fire, thus leaving a terra cotta vessel with a basketry pattern on the outer side as though imprinted from a mould; whether this be true or not it is a short step to develop from pattern effects accidentally achieved in the making of a pot, to ones deliberately formed by impressing it with a finger nail, corn cob, or roulette. The engraving of pattern with a sharp point was developed simultaneously, and in their simplest forms such patterns may cover the whole surface of a pot (Plate LXXa, b).

More formal use will be made of such decoration through the alternation of zones of plain and textured surface, or of areas in which the textural patterns differ; as the work reaches this stage it is not always easy to differentiate between what we have called texture pattern and geometrical design (Plates LXXc, LXXIa, b).

When we turn to decoration carried out on such materials as wood and calabash, ivory or metal, we find that the tendency is either to use texture pattern to fill up the background against which the forms of men or animals are set or to keep the background plain and to cover the forms with fine patternwork often representing the texture of clothing, animal pelts, or fish scales. At other times these texture patterns on the figures are entirely unrepresentational and merely serve to give continuity across the areas in relief; when background pattern is used it, in its turn, may be either completely non-representational or may consist of simple repetitions of floral or other symbols

MOTIFS IN AFRICAN DESIGN

(Plates XLIXb, LIV, LVb, c, LVI, LVIIIb, LX, LXI, LXIV, LXVI, LXVIII, LXIX).

REPRESENTATIONAL FORMS

Proverbs, allegories, adages and wise words form a backcloth to African thought, and both the myths and legends of the tribal past and the prestige of the reigning chief or king are summed up in aphorisms or visual symbols. It is this which gives us the key to much of African design. Most of the traditional pattern motifs of the various tribes had originally a symbolic or allegorical meaning. The initial intention of the craftsman when he carved or embroidered some animal or hieroglyphic was not to decorate his handiwork, not to depict some animal of which he was particularly fond, not even to make some mighty fetish, but to record a pictorial statement of an idea. The meaning may have been clearly stated or abstruse, it may have been kept secret to a privileged few, and in course of time it may have been completely forgotten, nevertheless it was the original reason for his act, we might call it the motive of the motif.

In this the African does not stand alone. To quote Ethel Lewis,[1] who has written an interesting account of the use of symbolism in textile design throughout the world, from the early civilizations through Europe, the Orient, and South America, down the ages, 'The patterns created in Egypt were distinctive though evolved in the same way as practically all early design. They grew from the need to represent in some way certain religious symbols. Carlyle has described decoration as the first spiritual want of man. And from that early need right down to our own times ornament has served as an expression of life. There is a story in each pattern, for every bit of ornamentation is a symbol of something, and each symbol is a record of history or experience.'

In monographs on specific examples of African design, such as wall painting or textile printing, one reads that modern work in the particular medium is representational while older examples are usually of geometrical pattern. It is very possible that in its early stages the older work was also as representational as its maker wished it to be, but that through successive copying and stylization it became reduced to a geometrical symbol accepted and understood in its own day but unintelligible to us now. The unravelling of the meaning of these African symbols is a task which we must leave to the ethnologist; and it can only be based upon many years of study sympathetically undertaken in all parts of the continent. Even so, it is doubtful whether at this late stage we shall ever be absolutely sure of all the interpretations which we are given. For even such reputable authorities as the late R. S. Rattray, and Eva Meyerowitz, may come to

---

[1] Ethel Lewis, *The Romance of Textiles*. New York, 1953, p. 5.

different conclusions as to the ideas behind such motifs as those cut on the stamps used in printing Adinkira cloths. Rattray[1] believed that the Ashanti borrowed these motifs from the amulet symbols used by the Arabs from the north but renamed them giving them a local historical, magical or allegorical significance; while Mrs. Meyerowitz[2] fits a number of them into an elaborate scheme representing different aspects of the Creator, adding a warning that although the real meaning of the symbols is known in secret by the craftsmen and their descendants, they are used freely and often other secondary meanings have been substituted for the original ones. Both these authorities may well be right, and one set of meanings may be secondary to the other, but it is obvious that for the amateur who has not studied the subject on the spot, any attempt at exegesis is fraught with danger. Happily the designer's field of study is something other than the interpretation of the content of these symbols, for his sphere is the appreciation of the form in which they are depicted, and although his task will be made both lighter and more interesting by all that he can learn of the meaning which they hold, yet their initial value for him lies in their visual appearance.

In the decorative art of certain parts of Africa, notably that of the West Coast Kingdoms, we find much use is made of both human and animal forms, which are depicted in every degree of stylization from almost naturalistic representation to the near-abstract symbol. No purpose would be served by illustrating these forms and symbols in a haphazard fashion from many different tribes, and it has seemed best to concentrate on the work of one or two regions where their use has been most highly developed. In many cases it would seem that these motifs are used to portray the glory and honour of the tribe as personified in the ancestors or living rulers. These rulers are often represented in the form of animals to whom various approved characteristics are traditionally ascribed. The art of Dahomey affords a most excellent example of such a form of analogous representation. There, in bas-reliefs of clay which decorated the palace walls, and in appliqué hangings, umbrellas and banners, as well as in work in other media, the great deeds and victories of the kings, their glory and their powers are all set out in symbolic form. During the course of his reign each king acquired a series of praise-names which referred to an existing proverb or one which was coined to describe some incident in his life. Thus when the king Gezo supplanted his brother Adaza it was said: 'The horse carries a bit which the ox cannot carry,' and this found visual expression in the head of a horse wearing a bit of iron. Other such representations are a draped buffalo—'The cloth which falls on the buffalo's neck cannot be

[1] Rattray, *Religion and Art in Ashanti*. Chap. XXV.
[2] Meyerowitz, *The Sacred State of the Akan*. Chap. VI.

E*

removed'; a fish—'the fish who refuses the net cannot re-enter'; or a young lion who spreads terror abroad directly he has cut his teeth. Sharks, crocodiles, dogs, panthers, hornbills, toads, pythons and many other animals, birds and reptiles are used in a similar way.[1] In many cases one motif cannot carry the whole content of a proverb or a praise-name or represent the victorious action of the king in battle, so a whole panel is constructed of motifs which must be read together to understand the analogy (Plates V, XXV).

Another form of ornamental art carried out by the Dahomean people is that of calabash decoration. According to Herskovits[2] one type of elaborately decorated calabash is sent, with a suitable gift inside it, by a young man to the girl who has won his heart. Just as the royal bas-reliefs and appliqué cloths depict in allegorical form the glories of the kings, so these love tokens convey through groups of symbols, which represent well-known aphorisms, the state of the young man's affections. In these birds, animals, fish and serpents are represented together with numerous other objects such as stylized human faces or hands, palm trees, pots and knives.

The Dahomean calabashes illustrated in this book come from the collection made by the Dakar–Djibouti mission in 1931, and have been described by Griaule and Dieterlen[3] who state that they are to be found in huts and market places, but give no explanation of any allegorical meaning. Both these writers and Herskovits say that the use of the whole human figure in such calabash decoration is extremely rare (Plates XLVII, XLVIII, XLIXa).

Except for variations which are naturally due to the use of different materials and techniques, the treatment of natural forms in all these branches of decorative design in Dahomey is somewhat similar. The animals, and human figures where they are used, are first thought of as a solid silhouette, portrayed as naturalistically as is consistent with the artists' purpose. That is to say, in the bas-reliefs and appliqué cloths where the aim is chiefly descriptive and pictorial, liberties will be taken with the total size and relative proportions or stance of a figure or animal if by so doing the conception of grandeur or power can be enhanced. In calabash decoration, on the other hand, where the feeling for ornamentation is stronger, the animal forms may be elongated, compressed or distorted to fit them within the shape of the panel allotted to them, and the surface will be

[1] Mercier, *Etudes Dahoméennes*. V.
See also Herskovits, *Dahomey*. Vol. II, pp. 328 et seq.
Waterlot, *Les Bas-Reliefs des Bâtiments Royaux d'Abomey*.
[2] Herskovits, *Dahomey*. Vol. II, pp. 344 et seq.
[3] Griaule et Dieterlen, 'Calebasses Dahoméennes', *Journal de la Société des Africanistes*. Tome V. Fasc. II. 1935.

broken by bold pattern. Yet in both classes of work the subjects are kept as separate compact masses silhouetted against a plain ground.

When we turn to consider the use of animal and human forms in the art of Benin we find a completely different approach. Let us first try to make a composite picture of the actual appearance of the king and his courtiers from the records of the early explorers, for comparison with their representation in metal, ivory or wood.

'On entering the apartment I perceived his majesty; a fine, stout, handsome man, with somewhat of kingly dignity about him. . . . Several chiefs, in full dress, surrounded him, beside a bodyguard on either side, with drawn swords. On my approaching him, he held out his arm, which the three young princes stepped forward and supported.' Fawckner. 1825.

'Lastly came the king, supported by two men, who led him to the wooden bench upon which a mat had been placed, disposed his loin cloth and held both his arms.' Burton. 1862.

'He [the Captain of war] was standing in the upper alcove with two attendants gingerly supporting his coral and iron braceletted arms, which hung down loose and away from his sides. The general effect of his attitude upon a newcomer was that of a fainting man being caught in the act of falling . . .' Burton. 1862.

'The rich among them wear, first, a white calico or cotton cloth, about one yard long and half as broad, which serves them as drawers; over that they wear a finer white cotton dress, that is commonly about sixteen or twenty yards long, which they wind very neatly round the middle, casting over it a scarf of about a yard long, and two spans broad, the end of which is adorned with fringe or lace . . . the upper part of the body is generally naked.' Nyendael. 1704.

'The nobles were bare to the waist, save for a few strings of coral beads of no large size. Below the waist they wore very full petticoats.' Punch. 1889.

'He [a court official] was curiously habited, wearing a sort of short petticoat from the waist down to the knees, composed of a cloth very much valued by them, resembling our white bunting. This encircled his loins, and was set off like an ancient dame's hooped petticoat; the upper part of the body was naked, as well as the legs and feet.' Fawckner. 1825.

'He [the king] wore a net shirt of which each knot was furnished with a coral bead; it weighed more than twenty pounds.' Landolphe. 1787.

'The "Big men" had each his anklets and collar of coral, a very quaint decoration, composed of pieces of about one inch long, and so tight strung that it forms a stiff circle about a foot in diameter.' Burton. 1862.

'The chief's head was covered with coral beads, thickly strung on his black curly wool; his neck, ankles and wrists were also encircled with a profusion of strings of coral.' Fawckner. 1825. He also noted that besides the necklace which the king wore on state occasions he also wore a belt of coral.

[a noble] 'held an *ebere* in his hand which he kept twisting round.' Punch. 1889.

'In his hand he held a fan made of leather . . . to keep off the flies and protect him from the rays of the sun.' Fawckner. 1825.

'It was always quite the thing for an African potentate to have at least two slaves fanning him.' Punch. 1889.

When, after having read these descriptions,[1] we look at the bronze plaques representing the king and his courtiers, either with naked torsos and 'full petticoats' or with a net shirt covered with coral beads; with their chokers, armlets and anklets of coral; their fans and *eberes*: and note how the attendants are grouped about the king, fanning him and protecting him from the sun and supporting his arms, we tend to say that this is pure naturalism, with no attempt at symbol or stylization. Not only is every detail of dress meticulously recorded, but many figures break away from the position of frontality and present a side or even three-quarter view. Other works representing Portuguese, or African scenes apart from court life and people, are even more naturalistic. Yet in the midst of all this seemingly straightforward representation we perceive a strong symbolic element which is fitted in with no sense of incongruity. On some carved tusks the king's legs become a pair of mud fish curving upwards and ending in a head, on a plaque two snakes sprout from the nostrils of a human face, or the trunk of an elephant ends in a human hand. It is this dualism of the lifelike and the fantastic at one and the same time which is so remarkable in Benin art.

The mud fish element, together with serpents, double-headed birds, and other fantasies, must be fitted into Benin mythology; for they doubtless make reference to the gods; but there is one interesting stylization which has no supernatural meaning and has come about from a straightforward kind of shorthand. In the bronze plaque representing a Portuguese, Plate LXIXb, the head is shown in a most naturalistic way. The helmet has a broad brim, the hair is long, and combed downwards and outwards straight to the shoulders, and the beard ends in three points. In the version on

[1] All quoted Ling Roth. *Great Benin.*

70

the small plaque, Plate LXVId, some stylization has already taken place. The helmet has become a jaunty hat with up-turned brim, and the hair ends in a large curl on each side of the face. Finally the very formalized motif which is repeated over the blade of the *ebere* in the same plate has taken the elements of hat, hair and beard and turned them into a symbol for a Portuguese which we recognize only through having studied it in the earlier stages. This is an excellent example of the reduction of a natural representation to a completely stylized symbol (Plates LIXd, LXIV, LXVb, c, d, LXVI, LXVIII, LXIX).

In both the Dahomey and Benin work representational forms make up the chief part of the design. They are usually arranged in panels framed by borders of geometrical pattern and must be considered to have a literary as well as a decorative value. A somewhat similar approach can be seen in the wall paintings, wood and ivory carvings, printed cloths and metal work of other tribes illustrated here (Plates I, II, III, LII, LVIII, LXVa).

Then comes work in which human and animal forms seem to hold a less significant place, and are used either as symbolism or for their purely decorative value as a part of a general scheme of design (Plates XIc, XVIIc, XXXIIId, XLIII).

Still further developed are the motifs which obviously have some symbolic meaning or reference, but which have to be interpreted to all but the initiated (Plates VIIIb, XIII, XIVb, XXVIII); and finally those forms which to all intents and purposes appear to be purely geometrical. In all representational design animal motifs seem to predominate, followed by representations of the human figure and certain types of objects, while the use of floral forms is remarkable for its absence.

SYMBOLIC AND GEOMETRICAL PATTERN

In considering the use of geometrical and symbolic pattern in African design it has seemed more profitable to restrict ourselves in a similar way to that taken when studying human and animal motifs, and then to consider one or two areas where it is possible to find a fairly full account of its use. For this purpose we have taken the work of the Bushongo and neighbouring peoples of the central Congo.

When we come to analyse the pattern motifs in Congo embroidery and wood carving we find that it is not possible to work out any clear scheme of classification. Torday and Joyce, who made a very thorough study of the subject in 1910, said that the people themselves found it very difficult to name even well-known patterns with which they were quite familiar, and when they tried to do so, many arguments occurred, so that the matter had to be referred to expert craftsmen. The cause of their difficulties was that, unlike the European who regarded a pattern as a whole, the Bushongo appeared to break it up into a number of different elements and arbitrarily chose one to give the name to the whole design. This resulted in patterns which to us would appear to be quite dissimilar, being called by the same name; while others which we would consider similar were regarded as having no relationship at all to one another. Again, identical patterns were used in wood carving, and in tattooing the body, and in embroidery; and as both tattooing and carving were the prerogative of the men while embroidery was that of the women, the different sexes were likely to pick out different motifs as the key to the whole design, with the result that the same pattern would receive different names from each.

A very large number of the motifs are basically built up from interlacing pattern, and Torday and Joyce have attempted to elaborate the various stages through which they have passed, from the genuine technical necessities of weaving to their present form in embroidery and wood carving. The twisting and knotting of string in net making might seem an even more obvious source for certain of these patterns, especially as many riverine tribes use, and presumably make, large fishing nets. Another probability is that some are derived from the drawing games played by the young children of the tribe. These games consisted in drawing certain traditional designs in the sand in such a way that the whole figure was drawn in one continuous line without raising the finger from the surface. When the sand was damp the first part of the line would be eradicated in places by the crossing of later portions. This method of drawing would not result in a regular under-over, over-under, form of interlacing but would at least suggest the possibilities of such treatment. Similar games of pattern drawing with one continuous line are reported from Angola.

Other motifs in Congo pattern are derived from triangles, lozenges and so on; while from the names given to others it seems likely that they derive from old stylized representations or symbols. Such are 'Kanya's fingers', 'the drum of Mikope', 'Buffalo horns', 'the stones', 'the back of the wild cat', and 'the Chameleon's footsteps'.

Let us try to identify some of the patterns shown in our illustrations. Perhaps the most commonly used motif in Bushongo design is *Mbolo*. This would appear to be derived from the straightforward interlacing, as in weaving, of two pairs of strands, the four points of crossing being the essential element of the motif. The ends of the strands may be joined together in various ways, forming complete motifs such as are found carved on the lids of boxes, or embroidered in small sections of the pile cloths; or alternatively the interlacing may be continued as a long band of pattern on both carving and embroidery. The first type of *Mbolo* can be seen in three panels of Plate

72

XXb (1), on the right hand side of XXb (2), and in Plate XXb (3), where it forms pairs of oval links as a small central motif in parts of the pattern. The second type is shown in Plates XXb (6), XXI (8), and LIVd. Other variations will bear names, such as *Mongo*, the knee illustrated in Plate XXI (9), where the lighter portion shows the pattern element. *Mbolo* is one of the named motifs used in the sand-drawing games played by children which have been mentioned above.

Another motif, or set of allied motifs, arises from the twisting together of two cords. In this simple form it is called *Namba*, the knot. But the identification of this motif is just as confused as that of *Mbolo*. Apparently the cords in *Namba* should lie close together, forming no open loops between the twists; if they do leave such gaps the pattern becomes *Nyinga*, the smoke; and if the twists are accentuated into a very sharp angle and the gaps are also noticeable it is known as *Nemo Kanya*, the fingers of Kanya. Unfortunately, we have no example of this simple form of *Namba* in our illustrations, although the curvilinear interlacing pattern on the body of the pot shown in Plate LVI would appear to fit the description. According to Torday and Joyce, however, this pattern when used in wood carving by the men is called *Buina* because of its resemblance to the curved blade of the knife which they use. The angular *Nemo Kanya* is shown in Plate XXI (11).

A further state of confusion is reached when we learn that virtually any other form of twisted cord might be called *Namba*. The continuous single loop twisted on itself which we see in Plate XXb (3 and 5), is *Namba*, and so are many representations of twists and knots which would definitely seem to be based on netting and which are carved freely in the decoration of wooden vessels.

It would be fruitless in a book on general design to attempt to unravel further complications in the pattern names of the Bushongo; our purpose is served once we have realized that there is no easy road to recognition or understanding. Certain patterns, however, are easy to pick out although the connection between their name and their appearance may be quite obscure. Such are *Mosala Baba*, the feathers of Baba, shown in XXb (4), and XXI (12), where a group of four right-angled triangles are fitted together at their apex. The chevron pattern is known as *Mamanye*, the stones, and is illustrated here in Plate XXI (3).

Finally come a few in which the allusion conveyed by the name is fairly clear. Of these the most obvious is *Mayulu*, the tortoise in Plate XXI (5), suggested by the tortoise-shell; *Ikunji*, the eye, Plate XXI (7), where the triangular space suggests the subject; and perhaps *Lori Yongolo*, the feet of the chameleon, Plate XXI (10), conveys rather well the creeping gait of its namesake. It is interesting to compare these names with those of a very similar type given to the plaited matting patterns of Zanzibar

(Plate XIII); in both cases the pattern would appear to have first been made for technical or decorative reasons and named afterwards when the resemblance to an object was noticed.[1]

Although written over sixty years ago, Haddon's *Evolution in Art* must still be considered one of the classics on this subject, and nothing could sum up better the points which we have put forward here than two widely separated quotations from that book: 'By carefully studying a number of designs we find, providing the series is sufficiently extensive, that a complex, or even an apparently simple pattern, is the result of a long series of variations from a quite dissimilar original. The latter may in very many cases be proved to be a direct copy or representation of a natural or artificial object. From this it is clear that a large number of patterns can be shown to be natural developments from a realistic representation of an actual object, and not to be a mental creation on the part of the artist. There are certain styles of ornamentation which, at all events in particular cases, may very well be original, taking that word in its ordinary sense; such, for example, as zigzag lines, cross-hatching and so forth. The mere toying with any implement which could make a mark on any surface might suggest the simplest ornamentation to the most savage mind. This may or may not have been the case, and it is entirely beyond proof either way, and therefore we must not press our analogy too far. It is, however, surprising, and it is certainly very significant, that the origin of so many designs can now be determined, although they are of unknown age.' 'In studies such as these, the investigator should refrain from theorizing as far as possible; it is a dangerous game, for more than one can play at it, and the explanation is as likely to be wrong as right. The most satisfactory plan is to gather together as much material as possible, and it will generally be found that the objects tell their own tale, and all that has to be done is to record it.'

[1] The whole of this section is based on the very full account given in 'Notes ethnographiques sur les peuples communément appelés Bakuba'. *Annales du Musée du Congo Belge*. Series III. Tome II. Fasc. I, pp. 215 et seq.

Index

(Arabic numerals are page references, Roman numerals plate references.)

75

INDEX

INDEX

INDEX

78

Plates

PLATE I. WALL DECORATION

Top: Part of the painting of the Oku wall. By an Ibibio artist for Ibo tribe. Provenance, Bende Division. Nigeria.—This work was done by an Ibibio artist hired by the local people. It consists of 'a wall covered with gaily-coloured pictures showing in panels policemen, girls, cows, snakes, dancers and so on, singly and in groups. The borders between the pictures are often filled with patterns based on those of cloths. Each picture is complete in itself and there is no continuous story running through all, nor is there any connection in them with the customs or history of Olokoro; they are Ibibio. It is noticeable that everything is painted separately in a side view without one thing covering another. Several of the panels are very effective decorations in themselves, especially those with an arched decoration above the figures, and that of two dancers with long-tasselled headdresses and tails . . . The paintings are done on a clear white background— the old method used by the women of Bende was to polish the wall until the bits of mica in the mud made it shine with a golden sheen, and then to paint it with ochres, chalk and soot. At Okwu red and yellow ochres, pink clay, black and brown from a sap, and European manufactured washing blue and green powder paint have been used without any medium, such as gum, to make the pigments adhere'. See *Nigeria* 27. 1947.

Bottom: Wall painting from the Inre Court House, Provenance, Nr. Awka. Ibo tribe. Nigeria.—Here the stylized drawing of the men in canoes is very interesting. At the base three canoes are seen, viewed end-on; while above them the men are superimposed on what may be a bird's eye view of a canoe.

PLATE II. WALL DECORATION

Top: Wall painting. Southern Tanzania.—A painting of a legendary chief, Kifutumo, from a collection of wall paintings of the *Buyeye* and *Bugoyangi*, secret societies of snake charmers in Southern Tanzania.
See *Wall Paitings by Snake Charmers in Tanganyika*. Cory, London, 1953.
Bottom: Wall painting from an *Mbari* house. Near Aba. Nigeria.—These houses are filled with large mud figures and completely decorated with wall paintings. These consist chiefly of geometrical patterns, but also include panels containing stylized paintings of birds, animals and men, or highly intricate abstract pattern. The colours used are white, black, slate-grey, ochre, earth-red and washing-blue. This particular example with its patterning of dots and small circles gives the appearance of a mosaic. See *Nigeria* 49. 1956.

PLATE III. WALL DECORATION

Top: Wall painting. Probably Chokwe tribe. North East Angola.—A most comprehensive account of the wall paintings of some tribes of Angola is given by Redinha. (*Paredes Pintadas da Lunda.* Lisbon, 1953.) He tells of paintings made on the outer walls of huts, not by skilled craftsmen but by the ordinary people, for the sheer pleasure of decoration. Such work is of a very ephemeral character, and is technically amateurish; nevertheless it has vitality and a certain richness of colour and pattern. The subjects chosen are very varied, and consist of scenes from everyday life or legend. They are often schematic in their representation, and even when designs appear to be purely abstract, they prove to be crude attempts at topography. Amongst these people as elsewhere large integrated compositions are almost unknown, and the decoration consists in small isolated figures, or groups of figures or geometrical patterns.

Bottom: Wall painting. Provenance, Ekibondo Village. Niangara District. Bangba tribe. Uele. Congo.—In this small village, consisting only of some twenty huts, the old craft of wall painting has been revived by encouragement from the District Commissioner. This panel, representing a modern trend in wall decoration, is filled with fairly naturalistic snakes, fish, knives, and so on. Other similar ones show elephants, leopards and other animals, and men. All the elements, which are taken from well known stories, are placed side by side. As in most primitive art the figures are static, the body is presented frontally, the head and legs in profile. Each line or form is incised in outline on the wall and then filled in with colour. Colours used are ochre, white (kaolin) and black (charcoal, crushed with a certain leaf).

PLATE IV. WALL DECORATION

Top: Abstract wall painting. Provenance, Nyanza Province. Luo tribe. Kenya.—These were painted by a local craftsman on the walls of a schoolmaster's house between 1940 and 1945. Unfortunately no further information about them is now available. The designs are excellent.

Bottom: Symbolic wall painting. Provenance, Ekibondo Village. Niangara District. Bangba tribe. Uele. Congo.—This panel is a more ancient form of decoration than that shown in Plate III (*bottom*). It consists of abstract symbolic forms, which probably date right back to the religion of the Sudanic ancestors of this tribe. It is said to represent an old myth from the cult of the sun and the moon, the central rosette signifies the sun. The cross bands of pattern represent the moon, and the undulating lines joining them are 'the feet of the moon'. The sun is always present, but the moon walks with the rain and so must have feet. The motifs are welded together into a rich geometrical pattern.

PLATE V. WALL DECORATION

Top: Clay panel in bas-relief. 74 × 77 cm. Provenance, Palace of Agadja. Dahomey.—This naturalistic panel represents an allegory concerning the king Agonglo (1789–97). One explanation is that it is based on the saying, 'I am the pineapple against whom the lightning can do nothing'; signifying the pineapple growing beneath the palm which does not suffer even when the tree is struck by lightning. Another is that it refers to a proverb, 'The sheep do not eat the leaves of the palm tree'. The stylized representation of the palm tree shows a good sense of design.

Bottom: Clay panel in bas-relief. 73 × 75 cm. Provenance, Palace of Agadja. Dahomey.—This panel represents the conquest of the coastal territories and first contact with the people of Dahomey by the Europeans, who are represented by a seated Portuguese priest. The Dahomeans believed the Europeans could not walk as they always saw them seated. An extremely well designed panel.

PLATE VI. WALL DECORATION

Moulded decoration on the outer walls of houses in Bida, Northern Nigeria.—In this example the motifs are contained within panels. Imported plates and dish covers are embedded in various places to give colour to the design.

PLATE VII. WALL DECORATION

Moulded decoration on the outer wall of a house in Kano, Northern Nigeria.—The decoration covers the whole surface of the wall with no repetition of form except round the windows. Rich traders cover the front of their buildings with geometrical designs moulded with mud and covered with native cement from the dye pits, or with real cement. External decoration of this type is said to be of comparatively recent development, as until the end of the last century such patterns were only made on the interior walls of the houses.

PLATE VIII. WALL DECORATION

Top: Part of the vaulted ceiling in the reception room of the Emir of Kano. N. Nigeria.—Large coloured china plates are set in the mud at the intersection of the arches, like a boss. Interior decoration of this type preceded the exterior ornamentation of mud buildings at Kano. It was the work of women. See *Nigeria* 23. 1946.

Bottom: Coloured decoration on interior wall of hut. Hima tribe. Uganda.—Each of these motifs is symbolic, although the knowledge of the meanings of the symbols is fast dying out. Of these the following meanings are recorded. Top row reading from left to right: 1. The veil of modesty. (A veil made of strands of beads worn to conceal the face of a woman who worships the *Bacwezi* and who is possessed by a spirit. Her eyes must not be seen while she is in this condition.) 2. Two arrows. 3. Moons, the planet Venus, and smaller stars. 4. (*In centre to right of the veil.*) A crowd of warriors in formation. 5. ?. Bottom row: 6. 'The Patterns'. (These are put on men's arms when the rains break and the herds return from the search for water.) 7. ?. 8. A spiral hair style.

See Sekintu and Wachsmann, 'Wall Patterns in Hima Huts'. Uganda Museum, 1956.

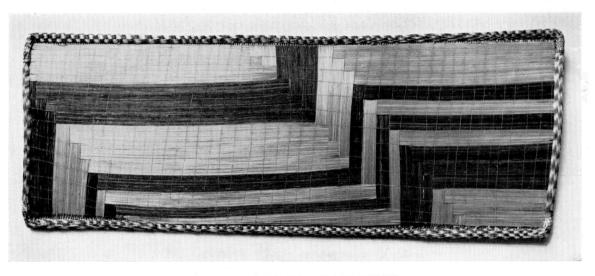

PLATE IX. WALL DECORATION

Top: Exterior wall of woven matting. Bushongo tribe. Congo.—Both interior and exterior walls of Bushongo huts may be covered with matting patterned in traditional design.

Bottom: Screen in sewn matting. 120 cm. × 45 cm. Tusi tribe. Rwanda. Collection Margaret Trowell.—A screen used to partition off the platform on which the milk pots stand in a Tusi hut.

PLATE X. PATTERNS ON MATS AND SCREENS

Top: Woven mat. 175 cm. × 110 cm. Provenance, Boma. Sundi tribe. Lower Congo. Musée Royal de l'Afrique Centrale.
—This woven mat has a warp of two colours, red-brown and purple, and is woven with a white weft which is floated behind and before a number of the warp strands so that the pattern can be seen in reverse on the other side of the mat.
Bottom: Sewn mat. Bushongo tribe. Central Congo. Musée Royal de l'Afrique Centrale.—This mat is made with a set of broad flat splints which are closely over-sewn with black and natural coloured raffia after the manner of coiled basketry. The reverse face can be seen rolled on the right hand side of the photograph. The motifs used are commonly found in Bushongo embroidery.

PLATE XI. PATTERNS ON MATS AND SCREENS

Top: Woven mat. Provenance, Cataracts. Lower Congo. Musée Royal de l'Afrique Centrale.—The weaving technique is clearly shown in this mat. The design appears in reverse, in white on black, on the other side of the work.

Centre: Woven mat. 171 cm. × 111 cm. Provenance, Cataracts. Lower Congo. Musée Royal de l'Afrique Centrale.— Technically this mat is woven in the same way as the one shown above. The human and geometrical motifs are more ambitious and better arranged.

Bottom: Woven mat. 159 cm. × 107 cm. Provenance, Cataracts. Lower Congo. Musée Royal de l'Afrique Centrale.—In the third example of this type of mat the bird motifs are used to make a definite repeat pattern.

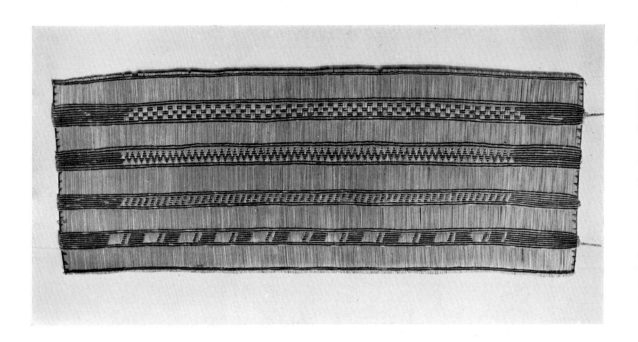

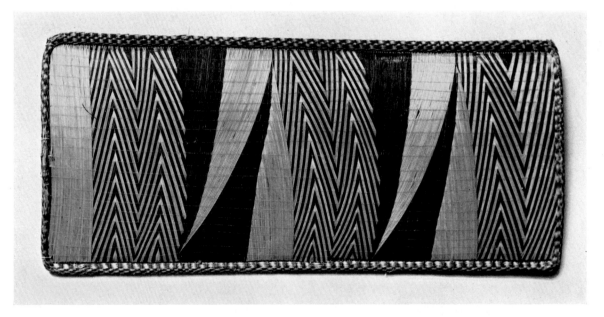

PLATE XII. PATTERNS ON MATS AND SCREENS

Top: Sewn mat. 108 cm. × 41 cm. Provenance, Mbarara. Hima tribe. Uganda. Uganda Museum.—The fine splints of the ground are sewn together by the black pattern work. This pattern is raised by a fibre cord under the stitching. The mat is worn draped over the head by an unmarried girl when leaving her own compound.

Bottom: Screen is sewn matting. 45 cm. × 95 cm. Tusi tribe. Rwanda. Collection, Margaret Trowell.—On top of a groundwork woven of flat splints the patterned covering of long black and natural coloured reeds is arranged and sewn in place with rows of fine fibre, the stitching being kept as invisible as possible. These screens are set up round the platform on which the sacred milk pots stand.

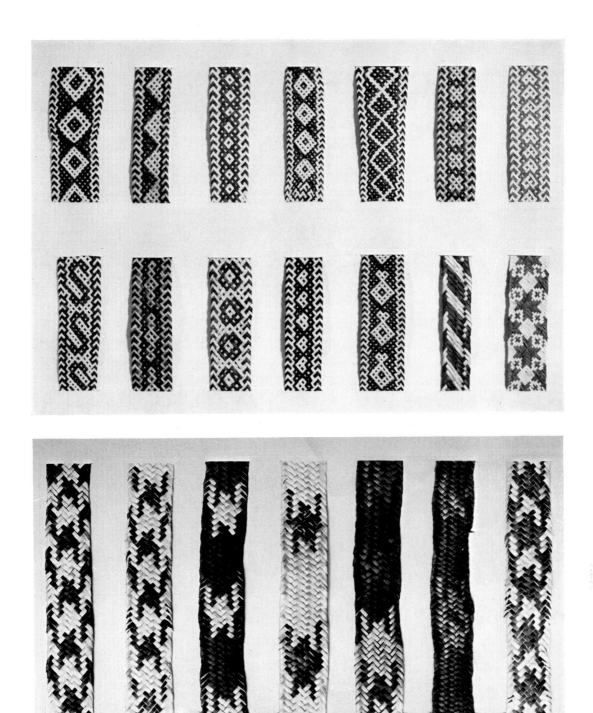

PLATE XIII. PATTERNS ON MATS AND SCREENS

Top: Set of patterns used in the making of plaited mats. Zanzibar. Collection, Margaret Trowell.—These mats are plaited in many bright colours, usually only one colour is used at a time combined with natural palm leaf. When the mats are made up the pattern motif forms an all-over pattern, or the decorated bands may be separated from each other by plain strips, or rows of different pattern may be sewn close together. The names of the patterns shown in this illustration are as follows (*reading from the left*): 1. The Window. 2. The Bat's Wing. 3. The Hen's Eye. 4. The Cow's Eye. 5. The Diamond. 6. The Cross. 7. The Heart. 8. The Snake. 9. The Bowtie. 10. The Lion's Foot. 11. The Fish Trap. 12. The Fish. 13. The Dog's Ribs. 14. The Starfish.

Bottom: Set of patterns used in the making of plaited mats. Nubian women in Uganda. Collection, Margaret Trowell.— Nubian women plait their mats with a double thickness of strands, working with one colour on top of another so that when the end of a plaited line is reached and the strands bent back to be worked in the opposite direction the colours are reversed. They rely on colour changes for the interest of their pattern rather than on the use of complicated motifs as can be seen from the sampler above, which contains seven variations on one basic pattern.

PLATE XIV. PATTERNS ON MATS AND SCREENS

Top: Prayer mat. Peace Memorial Museum. Zanzibar.—A very beautiful example of plaited matting. The broad strips of complicated pattern would entail a large number of strands in the plaiting.

Bottom: Prayer mat. Peace Memorial Museum. Zanzibar.—In this mat what appear to be Arabic characters have been used in certain stripes; their irregular form would involve very skilful arrangement of the plaited strands.

PLATE XV. TEXTILE DESIGN

Top: Woven cloths. Yoruba tribe. Nigeria.—These cloths are made of narrow strips sewn together.

Bottom left: Raffia woven mat. 69 cm. × 55 cm. No recorded provenance or documentation. Congo. Musée Royal de l'Afrique Centrale.—In both warp and weft black and white strands alternate, and are so woven as to give alternate vertically and horizontally striped squares; the squares themselves being in plain weave.

Bottom right: Silk Kente cloth. Nsuta. Ashanti tribe. Ghana. From the Beving Collection, late 19th or early 20th century. British Museum.—The cloth is made by sewing together a number of strips woven on a narrow loom. The common form of loom used by the Ashanti has two pairs of healds, one to weave the plain web and the second to produce the decorative pattern which is woven with additional wefts. These silk cloths are a blaze of brilliant colour—red, blue, green, black, white and yellow. Each design motif is named and has its own special significance.

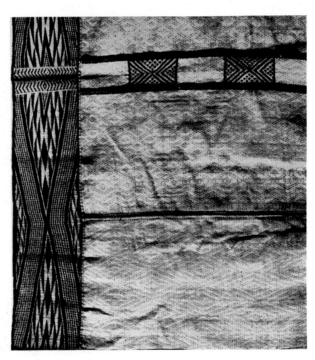

PLATE XVI. TEXTILE DESIGN

Top left: Loom for weaving raffia palm leaf fibre. Tetela tribe. Central Congo. British Museum.—The loom is provided with a heddle, shed stick and beater. (The latter standing vertically on the right in the photograph.) At the top of the warp can be seen some three down pattern rods threaded through the warp so that each may form the required shed for its place in the pattern. These rods are small in diameter and could not be used as shed sticks to open the sheds, so that it is probable that the weaver uses his fingers to trace down the openings to the weaving level of the texile. As each pattern rod is used it is withdrawn, and if required again replaced above the other rods in readiness for a repetition of the pattern.

Top right: Detail of woven raffia cloth. Kela tribe. Central Congo. Pitt Rivers Museum, University of Oxford.

Bottom left: Woven raffia cloth. 70 cm. × 38 cm. Jonga tribe. Central Congo. Musée Royal de l'Afrique Centrale.—This mat is typical of the type woven on the loom shown in *Top left*. The light design in red-brown and black on a natural ground gives a very delicate effect.

Bottom right: Woven raffia cloth. Mbun tribe. Kwango. Congo. British Museum.—The pattern of the side panels of this cloth shows the type of geometrical motifs which are used in African weaving. The central panels show two variations on the lozenge motif in diaper or one colour weaving.

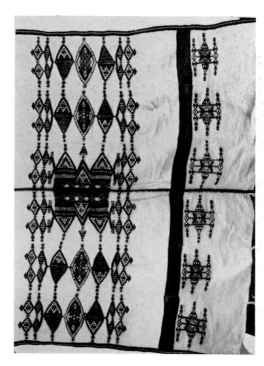

PLATE XVII. TEXTILE DESIGN

Top left: Woven cloth. Keta cloth. Ghana. Beving Collection, late 19th or early 20th century. British Museum.—This cloth is made up of two types of alternating narrow bands sewn together. The first is red crossed with dark blue, giving a purple effect, the second white. Both are decorated with stripes and other motifs including a bird and a fish woven with extra wefts.

Top right: Woven cloth. Probably Southern Nigeria. Beving Collection, late 19th or early 20th century. British Museum. —A cloth with alternating horizontal panels of stripes and various geometrical motifs in brocaded weave.

Bottom left: Woven cloth. Provenance, Bamenda. Cameroons. Probably from the Niger Delta region. Pitt Rivers Museum, University of Oxford.—A white warp with a thin blue thread every quarter of an inch. The pattern is brocaded, one motif is possibly a human symbol.

Bottom right: Detail of woven pattern on a blanket. Provenance, Lake Cuallando. Debo. Fulani tribe. Mali. Pitt Rivers Museum, University of Oxford.

PLATE XVIII. TEXTILE DESIGN

Woven cloth. Upper Senegal. Beving Collection, late 19th or early 20th century. British Museum.—A cloth made from strips woven on a narrow loom with a very intricate design in dark blue and white.

PLATE XIX. TEXTILE DESIGN

Top left: Detail of pile cloth. Probably the old kingdom of Congo. Lower Congo. Pitt Rivers Museum, University of Oxford.—The darker parts of this design are formed by embroidering the areas with finely shredded, dyed raffia, every stitch of which is cut off close to the surface giving a texture like pile velvet. In the lighter spaces in between the pattern is made by diaper weaving in natural coloured raffia. This cloth was collected before 1883, and is thought to have formed part of the Tradescant collection, acquired in the seventeenth century.

Top centre: Detail of pile cloth. Provenance, Boma. Probably Bushongo tribe. Central Congo. Pitt Rivers Museum, University of Oxford.—In this cloth, collected about 1910, the pile areas are made in the same way as in *top left*, while parts in between are embroidered with four rows of oversewing.

Top right: Detail of border of pile cloth. Provenance, Kasai area. Central Congo. Pitt Rivers Museum, University of Oxford.—This strip of border pattern shows the Pile cloth technique developed into the making of little bobbles of raffia; the bobbles are light and dark blue, warm yellow ochre and beige, while the ground is Indian red. The whole effect is that of a mosaic.

Bottom: Raffia pile cloth. 21 cm. × 32 cm. Bushongo tribe. Central Congo. British Museum.—Typical patterns found in Bushongo embroidery.

1 *Mbolo*   2 *Mbolo*   3 *Mbolo* and *Namba*

4 *Mosala Baba*

7   6 *Mbolo*   5 *Namba*

PLATE XX. TEXTILE DESIGN

Top: Embroidered raffia cloth. Bambala sub-tribe of Bushongo tribe. Congo. British Museum.—This cloth dates back to the 18th century. The cloths embroidered in this way, in contrast to those used for pile cloth, were very finely woven. Much of the work was done in a complicated form of chain stitch; and parts appear to be embroidered in a type of drawn thread work.

Bottom: Embroidered raffia cloths. Bambala sub-tribe of Bushongo tribe. Congo. British Museum.—Further examples of 18th century cloths. These cloths show examples of a number of traditional patterns; the names of those referred to in the chapter on geometrical pattern motifs are given above.

1

2

nye 3

4

vulu 5

6

7 *Ikunji*

8 *mbolo*

9 *mongo*

10 *Lori*
   Yongolo

11 *Nemo*
   Kanya

12 *Mosalo*
   Baba

PLATE XXI. TEXTILE DESIGN
Embroidered Cloths. Bambala sub-tribe. Bushongo tribe. Congo. British Museum.—Further examples of traditional
patterns motifs are shown here.

PLATE XXII. TEXTILE DESIGN

Top: Detail of embroidered robe. Provenance, Bida. Nupe tribe. Northern Nigeria. British Museum.—Part of a brilliantly embroidered robe in gold and silver thread on a scarlet ground.

Bottom: Detail of embroidered robe. Hausa tribe. Northern Nigeria. Pitt Rivers Museum, University of Oxford.—White embroidery on a blue ground.

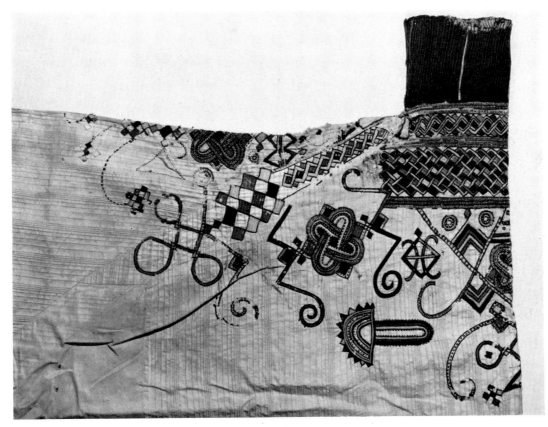

PLATE XXIII. TEXTILE DESIGN

Top: Embroidered robe. Bamenda. Cameroons. Pitt Rivers Museum, University of Oxford.—Embroidered in red, white and yellow cotton on a blue ground.

Bottom: Detail of embroidery on very wide trousers. Probably Hausa tribe. Nigeria. Pitt Rivers Museum, University of Oxford.—The 'cuff' of the garment is woven in red and buff stripes. The main part of the garment is cream embroidered chiefly in red with some blue, green, black and yellow. A far less formally arranged design than the one shown above.

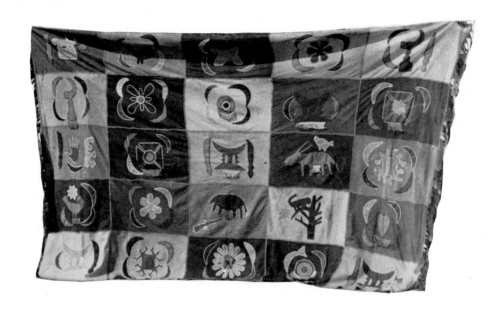

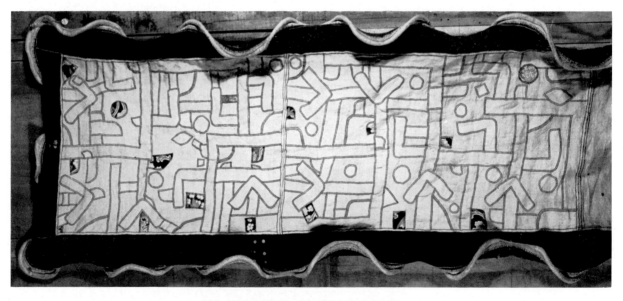

PLATE XXIV. TEXTILE DESIGN

Top: Appliqué cloth. An appliqué cloth of the Gyamanhene. Ashanti tribe. Ghana.
Bottom: Appliqué cloth. 161 cm. × 69 cm. Bushongo tribe. Congo. Musée Royal de l'Afrique Centrale.—A palm cloth with appliqué strips of the same material together with a few patches of imported prints and a border of pile cloth with insets of imported red fabric.

PLATE XXV. TEXTILE DESIGN

Appliqué cloth. 177 cm. × 107 cm. Provenance, Abomey. Fon tribe. Dahomey. Musée de l'Homme.—In this cloth the king is given an animal form symbolizing strength and is represented as far larger than his retainers and his enemies. Note that the retainers and the enemies have been cut from two patterns.

PLATE XXVI. TEXTILE DESIGN

Top: Painted barkcloth. 135 cm. × 130 cm. Mangbetu Tribe. Uele. Congo. Musée Royal de l'Afrique Centrale·
— A very freely drawn design with a curious H-like motif constantly repeated.
Bottom: Painted raffia cloth. 161 cm. × 99 cm. No provenance. Congo. Musée Royal de l'Afrique Centrale.—An
interesting design, or series of designs, are painted on the natural coloured ground of this raffia cloth. The solid forms
are outlined with a narrow border of dark grey and filled in with brown. Dark grey spots cover the lighter areas.

PLATE XXVII. TEXTILE DESIGN

Painted cloth. No provenance. Ghana. British Museum.—The cloth is of white drill, roughly painted with an elaborate design very reminiscent of the embroidered robes of the northern tribes of the West Coast. The solid forms are outlined in black and filled in with green, red and yellow. Much of the background is covered with black 'writing' patterns which would appear to have been done with a pen.

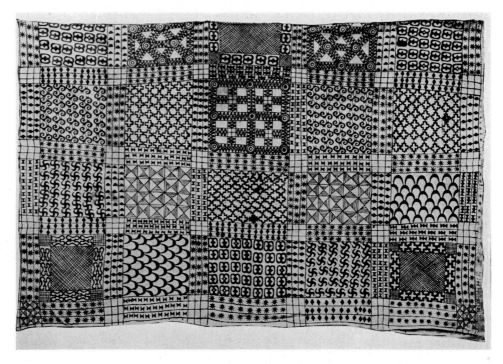

PLATE XXVIII. TEXTILE DESIGN

Top: Stamps used in printing *Adinkira* cloths. Ashanti tribe. Ghana. British Museum.—The stamps are cut from small pieces of calabash. Each one is named and has some symbolic meaning, some are the prerogative of the Royal household alone.

Bottom: Adinkira cloth. Provenance, Bonwere near Kumasi. Ashanti tribe. Ghana. British Museum.—This cloth, collected before 1934, shows the use of the stamp patterns illustrated above. The different motifs are usually printed in small panels either fitting closely together or separated by narrow bands of pattern as in this illustration.

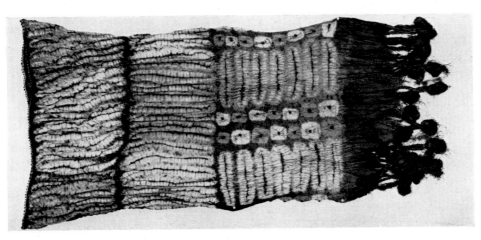

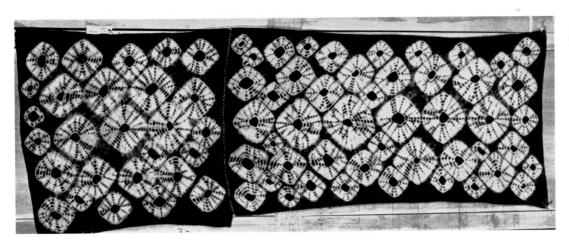

PLATE XXIX. TEXTILE DESIGN

Top left and top centre: Rope tie dyeing. Senegal. Beving Collection. British Museum.—The cloth is sewn and bound tightly together in parallel bands until it resembles a rope. When dyed and opened out the result is a series of horizontal undyed lines varying according to the closeness of the gathering and the thickness of the material.

Top right: Embroidered tie dyeing. Senegal. Beving Collection. British Museum.—The parts which are required to remain white have been closely oversewn in this specimen. The cloth will be dyed and the embroidery unpicked to get the desired effect.

Centre: Fine raffia cloth. Tie dyed. Ivory Coast. Musée de l'Homme.—This cloth appears to be plaited rather than woven, with the warp and weft threads on the bias as in certain basketry and mat-making techniques. It has been twice tied and dyed. The colouring is light yellow ochre, darker red ochre and black. The cloth has been left crimped and puckered.

Bottom: Tie dyed cloth. 150 cm. × 54 cm. Probably coastal region. Congo. Musée Royal de l'Afrique Centrale. —A very accomplished piece of tie dyeing in black and natural raffia colours.

PLATE XXX. TEXTILE DESIGN

Top: Zinc stencil used in resist printing. Yoruba tribe. Nigeria.—The starch paste is painted on to the cloth through the stencil and allowed to dry. The cloth is then dyed, when the parts covered with the paste are unable to pick up the colour. The paste is finally removed from the cloth, leaving the design white against a dark ground.

Bottom: Resist printed cloth with stencil. Yoruba tribe. Nigeria.—Here a cloth is seen after dyeing.

PLATE XXXI. TEXTILE DESIGN

Top: Cloth printed by the Discharge method. Design showing red on a black ground. Bambara tribe. Mali. Musée de l'Homme.—The cloth having been dyed dark brown or black by soaking in a concoction made from the bark or leaves of certain trees, the design is then painted onto the cloth in a mud probably containing iron acetate. When this is dry the design is painted over a second time with a local soap made from ashes and vegetable oils containing a large amount of potash which acts as a mordant. It is finally painted yet a third time with the mud used in the first coat and thoroughly dried in the sun. The dye is thus chemically removed from the cloth in the painted area so that when the mud has been chipped and rubbed away the pattern stands out light against the dark ground. In this cloth and in the one shown below from the same area the designs have much in common. Both are treated as line drawings, with no solid masses; and certain motifs such as the zigzag line, lozenge shape, and the main form which divides up the broad border on the right of each cloth are used in both. There is sufficient variation in the different borders and panels to avoid monotony.

Bottom: Cloth printed by the Discharge method. Design showing red-brown on a black ground. Bambara tribe. Mali. Sudan. Musée de l'Homme.—As above.

PLATE XXXII. TEXTILE DESIGN

Top: Cloth printed by the Discharge method. Bambara tribe. Mali. Musée de l'Homme.—Of the four cloths illustrated in this section this specimen is the most elaborate. Use is made of both solid light areas and fine line work, and the motif used in the squares of the central panel shows great variety of detail within its general uniformity. The same may be said for the other large motifs used in the borders.

Bottom: Cloth printed by the Discharge method. Bambara tribe. Mali. Musée de l'Homme.—The treatment of the pattern in this cloth is very similar to the one shown above.

PLATE XXXIII. ORNAMENTAL BASKETRY

Top left: Container of bark, covered with woven basketry. Height 31 cm. Diameter 27 cm. No provenance. Lower Congo. Musée Royal de l'Afrique Centrale.—In both this specimen and the next the container is made of bark, and the woven cover serves a decorative purpose only. Colouring black on a natural ground.

Top right: Container of bark, covered with woven basketry. No provenance. Lower Congo. Musée de l'Homme.— Colouring black on a natural ground.

Bottom left: Woven basket partly covered with more finely woven decorative outer layer. Height 21 cm. Diameter 37 cm. No provenance. Tanzania. Manchester University Museum.—In this case the supporting layer is itself made of woven basketry. Colouring black on a natural ground.

Bottom right: Coiled basket. Barotseland. Zambia. British Museum.—This large basket is decorated with geometrical pattern and birds and quadrupeds. Colouring black on a natural ground.

PLATE XXXIV. ORNAMENTAL BASKETRY

Top: Casket with decorative woven casing. No provenance. Probably Lower Congo. British Museum.—A very beautiful specimen of fine basketry which was acquired by the York Museum in 1827. Colouring black on a natural ground.

Bottom: Casket similar to the above. Length 43 cm. Height 32 cm. No provenance. Lower Congo. Musée Royal de l'Afrique Centrale.—Note the chevron pattern running round the body of the basket.

PLATE XXXV. ORNAMENTAL BASKETRY

Top: Three lidded baskets. Height I, 16 cm. (including lid); Height II, 13 cm. (including lid); Height III, 15 cm. (including lid). Tusi tribe. Rwanda. Musée Royal de l'Afrique Centrale.—The first and third of these baskets are woven, each in a different weave, the second is in coiled basketry.

Left centre: Woven stand for milk pot. Height 7 cm. Nyoro tribe. Uganda. Uganda Museum.—The pot stand is of coiled basketry with a very finely woven cover in red, black, and natural colour fibre.

Bottom left: Woven stand for milk pot. Height 9 cm. Nyoro tribe. Uganda. Uganda Museum.—The pattern in this pot stand is in natural, black and rich purple.

Bottom right: Two baskets. Height I, 17 cm.; Height II, 42 cm. (including lid); Tusi tribe. Ruanda Urundi. Musée Royal de l'Afrique Centrale.—The first of these baskets is woven, the second in coiled basketry. Both are patterned in black and natural colours.

All the small baskets and pot stands shown on these plates are of extremely fine and delicate workmanship.

PLATE XXXVI. ORNAMENTAL BASKETRY

Top left: Lidded basket. Provenance, Kwango area. Mbun tribe. Congo. British Museum.—The decorative interest of this basket lies in the use of different types of weave for the lid, the patterned band, and the base, with the raised bound bands dividing one area from another. The basket is all in natural colour.

Top right: Basket. Provenance, Kwango area. Mbun tribe. Congo. British Museum.—As in the previous basket, decorative interest is achieved by the method of construction alone, the vertical splints being held in place by a broad band of weaving round the centre which contrasts with the more open effect above and below and in the triangle left uncovered in the middle of the band.

Bottom left: Woven basket, with attached decorative band. Height 345 cm. Diameter at top 305 cm. Provenance, Kwango area. Mbala tribe. Congo. Musée Royal de l'Afrique Centrale.—The band attached to this basket serves the function of a handle, but has also been constructed with due regard to decorative values. Black design on natural colour ground.

Bottom right: Coiled basket on a wooden base. Provenance, Kasai. Bushongo tribe, Mbala sub-tribe. Belgian Congo. British Museum.—A royal basket said to contain the king's wisdom. The carved wooden base of this basket gives dignity to an otherwise not very outstanding design, although there is interest in the contrasting weight of the weaves in the pattern areas. Natural colour.

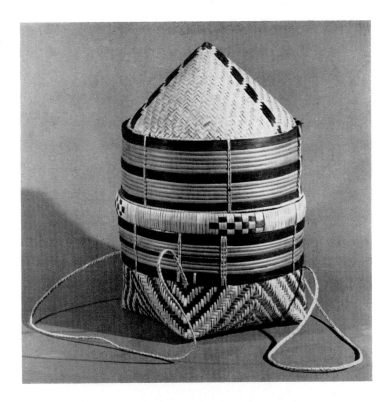

PLATE XXXVII. ORNAMENTAL BASKETRY

Top: Lidded basket. Height 36 cm. Diameter 24 cm. No provenance. Congo. Musée Royal de l'Afrique Centrale.
—This is a most interesting small basket. The square based basket becomes circular at the top, and further interest is added by the conical lid and the many bands of unwoven cane.
Bottom: Lidded basket. Height 35 cm. Diameter 38 cm. No provenance. Congo. Musée Royal de l'Afrique Centrale.
—The decorative portion of this basket is made of two bands of blackened wood carved in very low relief and attached to the base and lid.

PLATE XXXVIII. BEADWORK

Top: Beaded bag. Yoruba tribe. Nigeria. British Museum.—The colouring of this bag, presented to the Governor of Lagos at the beginning of this century, is far richer and more varied than that of modern beadwork.

Bottom: Beaded boots. Yoruba tribe. Nigeria. British Museum.—These boots have an interesting history. According to tradition Oduduwa, the first ruler of Yoruba, gave beaded crowns to his sixteen sons, who became rulers of the different Yoruba states. (See Mellor, 'Bead Embroideries of Remo', *Nigeria* 14, 1938, p. 154; also *Nigeria* 40, 1953, p. 306. (Photograph of beaded crown worn by the *Ataoja* of Oshogbo.)) The rulers of these states are alone entitled to wear such crowns, which had sixteen birds worked upon them. Besides the crowns were other articles of apparel, including boots. Later other chiefs pretended to equal rank, but their claims were disallowed. These boots, with eight stuffed beaded birds running up the front, belonged to a chief styled the Elepe of Epe, and were forfeited together with other articles when his claim was rejected. They were acquired by the British Museum in 1904.

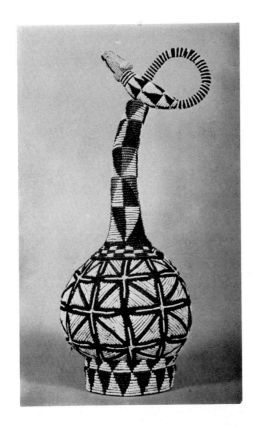

PLATE XXXIX. BEADWORK

Top left: Beaded covering of a calabash. Bali tribe. Cameroons. British Museum.
Top right: Beaded belts. Bantu tribes. S. Africa. British Museum.
Bottom: Bead covered cases. Heights, I, 19 cm.; II, 10 cm.; III, 11 cm. Tusi tribe. Rwanda. Musée Royal de l'Afrique Centrale.

PLATE XL. THE DECORATION OF HIDES AND LEATHER

Top left: Shaven Pattern. Subi tribe. Tanzania. King George V Museum. Dar es Salaam.—This pattern, on antelope skin, is formed by shaving away the hair in narrow lines.

Top right: Sheath with carved pattern. Height 45 cm. Bagam tribe. Cameroons. University Museum of Archaeology and Ethnology, Cambridge.—This pattern is cut out in low relief and emphasized by rubbing in a white chalky substance. *Bottom left:* Fan of cowhide with applied decoration. Benin. Nigeria. British Museum.—These circular fans of cowhide, ornamented with appliqué in red flannel and thin yellow skin, are mentioned frequently by early writers on Benin, and are represented in the hands of the King's retainers on many of the bronze plaques. Motifs used in their decoration seem to range from various symbols to leaf, animal and human forms.

Bottom right: Fan of cowhide with applied decoration. Provenance, Ogbe. Southern Nigeria. British Museum.— As *bottom left* above.

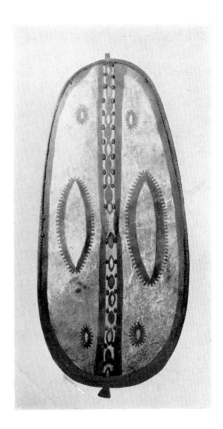

PLATE XLI. THE DECORATION OF HIDES AND LEATHER

Top left: Hide Shield. Height 110 cm. Masai tribe. Kenya. Manchester University Museum.—The decoration of these Masai shields is painted on in coloured earths.

Top right: Hide Shield. Height 125 cm. Masai tribe. Kenya. Manchester University Museum.

Bottom: Warriors with shields. Photograph by Hobley. Masai tribe. Kenya.

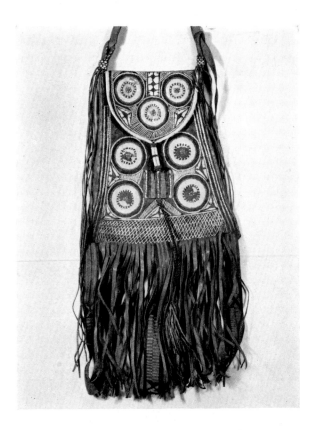
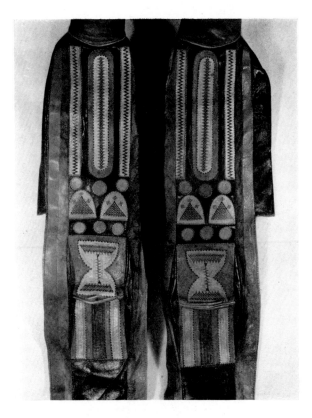

PLATE XLII. THE DECORATION OF HIDES AND LEATHER

Top left: Leather bag. Hausa tribe. N. Nigeria. British Museum.—The bag is decorated with appliqué and stitching in various contrasting colours, black, white and red on a dark tan background.

Top right: Part of pair of decorated leather boots. Provenance, Kano. Hausa tribe. N. Nigeria. British Museum. —The decoration of these boots is similar in technique to that of the bag on *left.*

Bottom left: Bag of the Shango cult. Yoruba tribe. Nigeria. British Museum.—Although the appliqué decoration of this bag has not the same technical precision as that of the two examples from Northern Nigeria, it is artistically more interesting in its irregularity.

Bottom right: Leather bottle cover. Sierra Leone. British Museum.—The cover is of dark red leather, the pattern being made by sewing in fine strips of dried leaf such as are used in mat making.

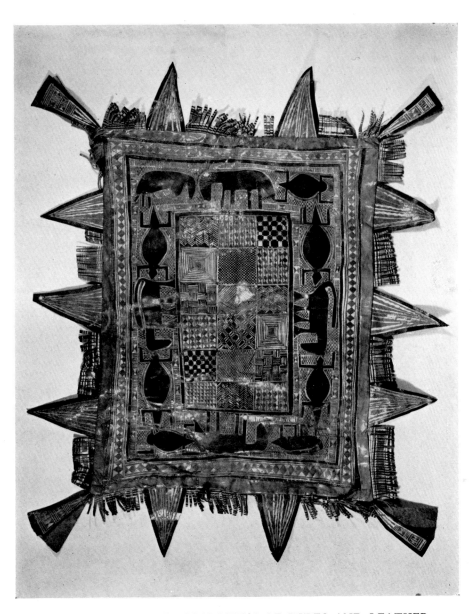

PLATE XLIII. THE DECORATION OF HIDES AND LEATHER

Cushion cover or mat. Provenance, Bida. Nupe tribe. N. Nigeria. British Museum.—This is a most interesting example of leatherwork, not only for its wealth of geometrical pattern motifs, but also for the use of animal, reptile and bird forms.

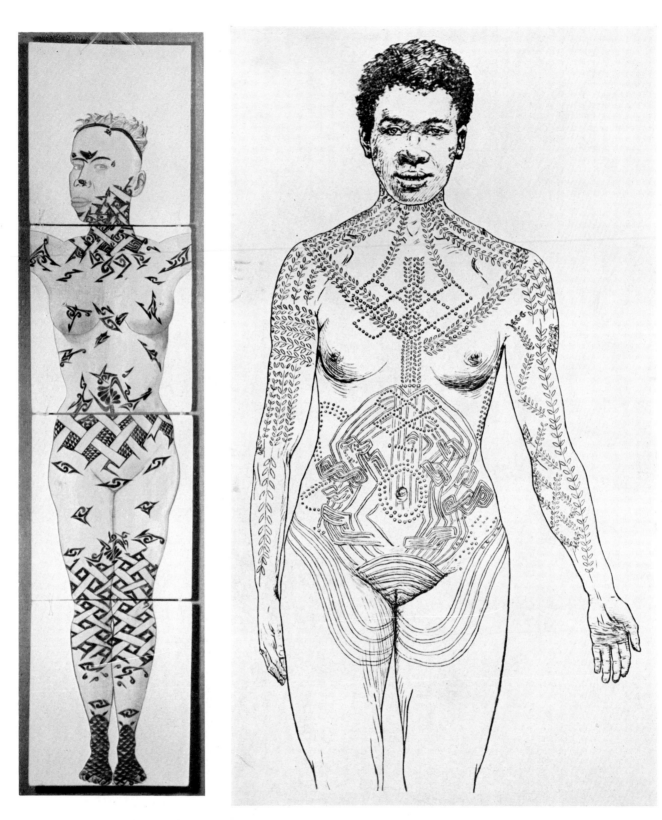

PLATE XLIV. CICATRIZATION AND BODY PAINTING

Left: Drawing showing correct placing of painted designs on the body. Tiv tribe. Nigeria.
Right: Drawing showing cicatrization patterns. Tetela (Sungu) tribe. Central Congo.

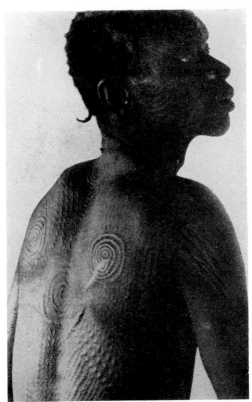
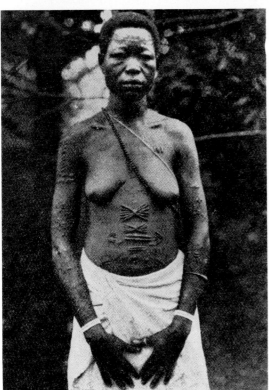

PLATE XLV. CICATRIZATION AND BODY PAINTING

Top left: Cicatrization pattern on woman's back. Mayombe tribe. Lower Congo.
Top right: Cicatrization pattern on woman's back. Nkutshu (Bankutu) tribe. Central Congo.
Bottom left: Cicatrization pattern on woman's abdomen. Tetela (Sungu) tribe. Central Congo.
Bottom right: Cicatrization pattern on the calves of the legs. Tiv tribe. Nigeria.

PLATE XLVI. CALABASH PATTERNS

Top: Carved calabash. Provenance, Lagos. Southern Nigeria. Manchester University Museum.—This calabash has been scraped before being carved with geometrical pattern. Portions of the pattern were then left white, while others were stained. The background of the pattern has been very deeply cut away.

Bottom: Carved calabash. Provenance, Ilorin. Northern Yoruba tribe. British Museum.—Another well carved calabash in which the shadows cast by the angular cutting give an added interest to the pattern.

PLATE XLVII. CALABASH PATTERNS

Scraped calabash lids. Bariba tribe. Dahomey. Musée de l'Homme.—In these calabash lids the background has been scraped away leaving the pattern motifs raised. Further contrast is given by the engraving of small texture patterns on the animal motifs contained within the panels, while treating the horizontal bands of geometrical pattern more broadly. Of these calabashes from Dahomey, Griaule and Dieterlen say that the panels are often filled with representations of animals or geometric pattern, sometimes with representations of objects, much more rarely with men. Herskovits also emphasizes the rarity of anthropomorphic representation. He says that the decorations convey messages to the initiated as clearly as would writing to the literate, and they represent symbolic stories, proverbs, or very often love messages, for they are presented by young men to the girl of their fancy. These calabashes from Dahomey are some of the most beautiful examples of calabash decoration and are clearly appreciated locally for aesthetic reasons.

PLATE XLVIII. CALABASH PATTERNS

Top: Two views of a scraped calabash drinking vessel. Dahomey. Musée de l'Homme.—This very fine example of a Dahomean calabash is decorated by the scraping technique, the cuticle of the background portions having been scraped away. The use of human motifs is somewhat rare; a third panel shows a bicycle. Each panel is well designed in itself; and the balancing of the figured panels with the plain portions, together with the borders at the top and bottom, give a very pleasing total effect.

Bottom: Two scraped calabash drinking vessels. Bariba. Dahomey. Musée de l'Homme.—These two very similar calabashes are also decorated by the scraping away of the background. In the panels can be seen stylized birds and animals together with various other symbols.

PLATE XLIX. CALABASH PATTERNS

Top: Scraped calabash bowl. Dahomey. Musée de l'Homme.—As plates XLV and XLVI.
Bottom: Scraped and engraved Calabash. Foulbe tribe. Cameroons. Musée de l'Homme.—This calabash from the Cameroons shows an entirely different treatment from the previous examples. In this case a very rich effect has been achieved through cleaning away the surface colour of the calabash in a few areas only, and covering even these with fine texture patterns. The free geometric design is excellent, every part being covered with interesting motifs skilfully combined into a satisfying whole.

PLATE L. CALABASH PATTERNS

Top: Decorated calabash. Probably Nupe tribe. N. Nigeria. British Museum.—A very fine example of calabash decoration. The texture pattern filling in certain portions of the design is reminiscent of basketwork.

Bottom: Three calabash lids. S.E. Nigeria. British Museum.—These calabash lids are excellent specimens of decoration by the scraping method. The groundwork is the natural deep sienna colour of the gourd, but the patterned portions have had the top layer of cuticle scraped off, leaving a white surface, which has then been stained in places with black.

PLATE LI. CALABASH PATTERNS

Top: Scorched and engraved calabash. Provenance, Bauchi town. Hausa tribe. N. Nigeria. British Museum.—This calabash would appear to have first been scraped, and then engraved by burning with an iron point. The wide black band has been scorched with a flatter tool.

Bottom left: Scorched calabash. Height 25 cm. Provenance, Kigezi. Kiga tribe. Uganda. Uganda Museum.—The black pattern is obtained by scorching with the blade of a knife or similar piece of metal. The curvilinear pattern is typical of the work of this tribe, but rare in many parts of Africa.

Bottom right: Scorched and engraved Calabash ladle. Probably Ibibio tribe. S. Nigeria. British Museum.—The flowing leaf pattern is typical of south-eastern Nigeria; see also Plate LXI.

PLATE LII. CALABASH PATTERNS

Top left: Calabash bottle engraved with a hot point. Hausa tribe. N. Nigeria. British Museum.—Although roughly executed the filling in of the panels is good.

Top right: Engraved calabash bottle. Kamba tribe. Kenya. British Museum.—This very decorative specimen is richly engraved with a very fine line. The engraved lines have been filled with some black material.

Bottom left: Engraved calabash bottle. Height 25 cm. Probably Lower Congo. Musée Royal de l'Afrique Centrale. —Loosely arranged and drawn, the drummers and dancers here make an interesting design.

Bottom right: Engraved calabash bottle. Tribe and provenance Unknown. British Museum.—The figures on this specimen are scattered about in a haphazard fashion. The chief interest in the work lies in the technique. The background has first been cut away leaving the figures in very low relief, and then engraved with groups of parallel lines; the figures are blackened by scorching.

PLATE LIII. CALABASH PATTERNS

Top left and right: Calabashes decorated with extraneous materials. Provenances unknown. (*Top left*) West Africa. British Museum.—The body of the calabash is the natural burnt sienna colour, with banks of black scorched pattern. These have been outlined with small white beads pressed into the skin of the gourd. (*Top right*) S. Africa.—In this case the pattern is stitched on to the calabash in brass and steel wire.

Bottom: Carved coconut. Provenance, Benin. Nigeria. British Museum.—This work in low relief much more resembles wood carving from the same area than calabash decoration.

PLATE LIV. DECORATION ON WOOD

Top left: Wooden drinking vessel. Height 19 cm. Bushongo tribe. Congo. Musée Royal de l'Afrique Centrale.—This specimen shows the use of a most interesting mixture of all-over texture pattern together with representational motifs in low relief, as the texture ornament is carried up on to the backs of the frogs.

Top right: Small wooden keg for gunpowder. Height 9 cm. Lower Congo. Musée Royal de l'Afrique Centrale.—In this example a geometrical motif of concentric squares has been cut so closely together that the pattern assumes a textural value.

Bottom left: Carved wooden cup. Provenance, Kasai. Bushongo tribe. Congo. American Museum of Natural History.—The interlacing straps and the spaces between them are filled respectively with parallel and cross-hatched lines forming an interesting texture pattern covering the whole vessel.

Bottom right: Carved wooden cup. Bushongo tribe. Congo. American Museum of Natural History.—In this cup more use has been made of spacing between the pattern bands. The pattern motif round the body of the cup is *Mbolo*.

PLATE LV. DECORATION ON WOOD

Top: Carved pattern on a head rest. Provenance, Mashonaland. Southern Rhodesia. British Museum.—These small head rests from Southern Rhodesia and Malawi demonstrate the African's ability to fit his pattern to whatever shapes he is presented with by the object he is decorating.

Bottom left: Wooden powder keg. Provenance, Loudima Niadi. Kamba tribe. Congo (Brazzaville). Musée de l'Homme.—The tall oval shapes fit the shape of the body, while the diamond pattern formed by engraved cross-hatching gives an interesting texture.

Bottom right: Wooden powder keg. No provenance. Lower Congo. Musée Royal de l'Afrique Centrale.—A more sophisticated and better executed example than *Bottom left,* but somewhat similar in design.

PLATE LVI. DECORATION ON WOOD

Wooden vessel. Provenance, Kasai. Congo. American Museum of Natural History.—An exceptionally lovely specimen of African carved decoration. The vessel itself is beautifully proportioned, and the closely incised texture pattern of the neck contrasting with the sweeping curves of interlacing pattern on the body emphasizes both the proportion and the shape. This pattern is known to the Bushongo tribe as *Buina*, and appears on many wooden objects.

PLATE LVII. DECORATION ON WOOD

Carved wooden door panel in low relief. Height 142 cm. Baule tribe. Ivory Coast. Collection. Mr. Josef Muller.—
A simple but extremely beautiful design. Note the contrast between the plain adzed wood of the background, with the
slight suggestion of waves, and the patterning of the fishes' bodies and fins.

PLATE LVIII. DECORATION ON WOOD

Left: Carved door panel. About 300 cm. high. Provenance, Ikare. Kabba Province. Eastern Yoruba. Nigeria. British Museum.—A good example of Yoruba door panelling with bands of processional figures divided by smaller bands of pattern.

Centre: Carved door panel. Provenance, Ijebu. Yoruba. Nigeria. British Museum.—A highly stylized design of figures and snakes. Note the small zig-zag pattern which is carried across each form.

Right: Part of a carved door-frame. Arab. Zanzibar.—Arab and Swahili carving was being replaced by the work of local Indians in Zanzibar early in this century, but some still remained. 'The chief carving designs' (in Arab and Swahili carving) 'are three in number: lotus derivatives, the rosette and a frankincense or date palm derivative. In every door-frame the designs on the two uprights spring at the foot from fish-like objects, figured apparently, in a head-downwards position, which are generally represented with a conventional scale pattern surface, and immediately below these fish-like objects there are sometimes figured two or three wavy lines, suggestive of the Egyptian hieroglyphic for water.' See Barton, 'Zanzibar doors' *Man.* June 1924, No. 63.

PLATE LIX. DECORATION ON WOOD

Top left: Carved wooden vessel. Height 22 cm. Bushongo tribe. Congo. Musée Royal de l'Afrique Centrale.—An elaborate and skilfully carved pattern.

Top right: Carved wooden drinking vessel. Height 19 cm. Bushongo tribe. Congo. Musée Royal de l'Afrique Centrale. —A rather unusual type of pattern covers this pot.

Bottom left: Carved wooden drum. Provenance, Kasai. Bushongo tribe. Congo. British Museum.—A very rich effect has been obtained here with the lattice work of knotted pattern known as *Namba* encasing the sun motif. The drum probably dates back to the reign of Bom Bosh, about the mid-seventeenth century.

Bottom right: Carved wooden drum. Provenance, Ijebu. Yoruba. Nigeria. British Museum.—The whole of this side of the drum is covered with a very stylized human figure; the legs becoming fish forms and turning upwards to be held by the hands; and hornlike appendages hanging down on either side of the large head, very common motifs in both wood and ivory carving from this district. Texture patterns cover most of the surface of the designs.

PLATE LX. DECORATION ON WOOD

Wooden milk pot. Height 34 cm. French Somaliland. Musée de l'Homme.—This milk pot is decorated in black and white work. The surface of the vessel is first blackened and then carved in low relief.

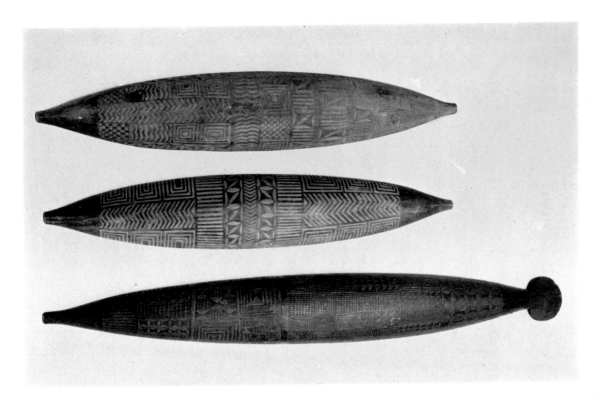

PLATE LXI. DECORATION ON WOOD

Top: Model canoes. Sierra Leone. British Museum.—The two top canoes shown here are in black and white work.
Bottom: Wooden fans. Ibibio tribe. S. Nigeria. British Museum.—These fans are decorated with patterns engraved with a hot metal point and blackened with a small flat metal tool. The flowing leaf-like forms are typical of the work of Eastern Nigeria.

PLATE LXII. DECORATION ON WOOD

Top: Two wooden shields and a decorated board used in dancing. Kikuyu tribe. Kenya. British Museum.—The shield on the left and dancing board on the right are in black and white work, while the central shield is painted.
Bottom: Three wooden shields. 1. Twa tribe. Rwanda. 2. Ganda tribe. Uganda. 3. Tusi tribe. Rwanda. British Museum.—Examples of painted shields.

PLATE LXIII. DECORATION ON WOOD

Top: Stool with wire decoration. Kamba tribe. Kenya. Manchester University Museum.—The wire used in decorating this stool has first been wound tightly round another piece of metal to twist it into a spiral, and then hammered into the surface of the wood which has been softened with oil.

Bottom: Stools with wire decoration. Kamba tribe. Kenya. British Museum.—These stools are decorated in a similar fashion to the one above.

PLATE LXIV. ORNAMENTAL IVORY CARVING

Top: Ivory bracelet. Provenance, Benin City. Probably Yoruba, Nigeria. British Museum.—The bracelet is carved in two layers from one piece of tusk; the inner one, which is decorated with drilled holes slipping round easily, but prevented from coming apart by two pegs of which the small bird at the centre base is one. The central figure of the king is the traditional representation carved symmetrically in a frontal position with legs developed into fish forms; while the other figures are freely and naturalistically carved.

Bottom: Ivory bowl. Height 12 cm. Provenance, Owo district. Yoruba, Nigeria. British Museum.—The figures on this carving are fairly naturalistic and clearly arranged in solid masses.

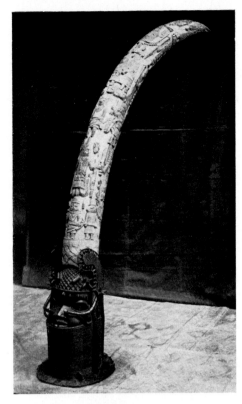

PLATE LXV. ORNAMENTAL IVORY CARVING

Top left: Ivory tusks. Provenance, Loango, Lower Congo. British Museum.—In these two tusks from the Lower Congo the figures are far more naturalistic and arranged in a more orderly way than those on the Benin tusk shown on the right.

Top right: Carved ivory tusk. Provenance, Benin. Nigeria. British Museum.—This tusk is typical of those found on the royal altars and burial grounds. A broad band of interlacing pattern surrounds the base, while above figures and emblems are arranged over the whole surface in an irregular but well-balanced manner. Both the stylized and naturalistic trends of Yoruba and Benin work can be seen here, the former in the representation of kings with supporting attendants on either side, and legs developed into fish forms; and the latter in the three quarter view of a horseman half-way up the tusk on the right-hand side.

Bottom, left and right: Carved ivory jug. Height 20 cm. Provenance, Benin. Probably Yoruba tribe. Nigeria. British Museum.—The metal rim and base, together with the wooden handle, are later additions. Of the motifs shown in these two views of the jug, the two headed bird in the upper stage of *bottom left,* the mud fish in the upper stage of *bottom right* and the elephant head in the lower stage of *bottom right* with the trunk divided into two arms of which the hands hold branches, are common symbols in Benin work, while the grazing antelope in the lower stage of *bottom left* is completely naturalistic.

PLATE LXVI. DECORATIVE METAL WORK

Top left: Armlet in repoussé work. Provenance, Benin. Nigeria. British Museum.

Top right: Brass *Ebere*. Provenance, Benin. Nigeria. British Museum.—These objects, usually about 90 cms. long, were not weapons but ornaments carried by Court officials. The one illustrated here is decorated with a repetition of a very stylized human head, probably meant to represent a Portuguese.

Bottom, left and right: Plaques decorated in repoussé. Diameter in each case 27 cm. Provenance, Benin. Nigeria. British Museum.—Thin brass sheeting decorated in repoussé. Probably late 19th century. Note that the figure *bottom left* is represented in the same way as that on the armlet (*top left*), while the head of the figure in *bottom right* is a rather more naturalistic version of that in *top right*.

PLATE LXVII. DECORATIVE METAL WORK

Top left: Cast brass *kuduo* or ceremonial vessel. Ashanti tribe. Ghana. British Museum.—In cast work the pattern is engraved in the wax.
The openwork stand has been brazed on to the vessel.
Top right: Repoussé brass vessel. Provenance, Attabubu, north of Kumasi. Ashanti tribe. Ghana. British Museum.—The design on this
vessel is punched into the brass and filled with a white substance.
Bottom left: Beaten gold Soul-Bearer's disc. Ashanti tribe. Ghana. British Museum.
Bottom right: Cast gold Soul-Bearer's disc. Ashanti tribe. Ghana. British Museum.

PLATE LXVIII. DECORATIVE METAL WORK

Top: Bronze plaque. Benin. Nigeria. British Museum.—This seventeenth-century plaque shows guards and attendants at the gate of the Oba's palace. Note the variety of pattern on the walls of the building, and attendants' shields and clothing.

Bottom: Bronze plaque. Benin. Nigeria. British Museum.—In this group representing the Oba with his attendants a great deal of naturalism has been attained while the convention of strict frontality is still adhered to. This combination of formal, symmetrical grouping, together with free rhythm, gives the work the quality of good design. The texture patterning of the clothing is even more interesting than in the previous example. The work is probably eighteenth century.

PLATE LXIX. DECORATIVE METAL WORK

Top: Bronze plaque. Benin. Nigeria. British Museum.—This plaque is probably seventeenth-century work, and one of the earliest styles known. It is considerably more rigid than those shown in the previous plate, both in the grouping of the figures and the pattern work.

Bottom: Bronze plaque. 48 cm. Benin. Nigeria.—The Portuguese shown in this plaque is most realistically represented. Special notice should be taken of his head, with its flowing hair and beard, long narrow nose and mouth, and helmet. Reference should then be made to the stylized types of Portuguese heads shown in Plate LXVI *bottom right and top right.* Here the characteristic features mentioned above are reduced to a decorative symbol.

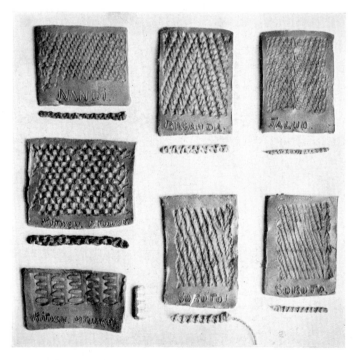

PLATE LXX. POTTERY DESIGN

Top left: Red earthenware water pot with impressed pattern. Height 35 cm. Nyoro tribe. Ugnada. Uganda Museum.—A very fine example of a roulette impressed pot.

Top right: Impressed pattern on a clay head. Tribe unknown. American Museum of Natural History.—No details are available of this work, but the decoration of the face with finger nail indentations is exceedingly interesting.

Bottom left: Buff earthenware pot decorated with impressed pattern. Height 25 cm. Budu tribe. Uele. Congo. Musée Royal de l'Afrique Centrale.—A biscuit coloured pot with broad bands of roulette impressed pattern outlined with an incised line. The interest of the design lies in the arrangement of the pattern bands which is most unusual.

Bottom right: Examples of roulettes with specimen impressions. East African tribes. British Museum.—The roulettes are placed below the clay slabs showing their impressions. That in the bottom left-hand corner is of wood, the rest of reed or fibre.

PLATE LXXI. POTTERY DESIGN

Top left: Cup or pot with incised pattern. Height 10 cm. No documentation. Nyoro or Hima tribe. Uganda. Uganda Museum.—
the groundwork of this pot is burnished black, and the finely incised pattern has been filled with white chalk or crushed shell.
Top right: Vase with incised and impressed decoration. Height 36 cm. Teke tribe. Lower Congo. Musée Royal de l'Afrique
Centrale.—The ground of the pot is a very light buff, and parts of the incised decoration have been filled in with a dark red.
Parts of the pattern are incised and the broken lines may be impressed with a metal ring.
Bottom left: Earthenware pot partially burnished, with incised and impressed decoration. Lower Congo. Musée Royal de
l'Afrique Centrale.—The neck and lower portion of this pot have been burnished, while the matt surface of the upper half of the
body is patterned. The horizontal grooves are deeply incised, and given interest by irregular verticals. The bands formed
between the grooves are further enriched by the lightly impressed pattern.
Bottom right: Earthenware pot, burnished and incised. Mayombe tribe. Lower Congo. Musée Royal de l'Afrique Centrale.—
The neck and upper part of the body, except for the patterned areas, are burnished a deep red, the lower part of the body has a
matt, unburnished surface. The pattern is incised with a deep, sharply cut line.

PLATE LXXII. POTTERY DESIGN

Top left: Black earthenware pot with moulded decoration. Provenance. Fumbam. Bamum tribe. Cameroons. Musée de l'Homme.—The stylized figures round the body of this pot, with the arms and legs forming a latticed pattern, are typical of the work of the Cameroons both in pottery and wood carving.

Top right and bottom: Three ceremonial vessels of black earthenware. Ashanti tribe. Ghana. British Museum.—The decoration of these pots combines moulded, impressed and incised work.

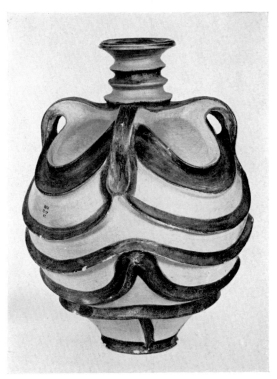

PLATE LXXIII. POTTERY DESIGN

Top left: Pot with moulded design. Provenance, Niger Delta. Ibo tribe. Nigeria. British Museum.—The lines of decoration of this pot have probably been pinched up while the clay was still soft, and then roughly impressed with a finger nail or piece of wood.

Top right: Pot with moulded decoration. Height 12 cm. No tribe or provenance. Congo. Musée Royal de l'Afrique Centrale.—This very well designed little pot is in a very light coloured clay, the raised pattern is simple and balanced.

Bottom left: Water pot with moulded design. Provenance, Inye. Northern Ibo tribe. Nigeria. British Museum.—The very large pot is covered with deep grooves and ridges which have been darkened with a slip of coloured clay.

Bottom right: Earthenware pot with moulded and impressed decoration. No documentation. Congo. Musée Royal de l'Afrique Centrale.—The grooved neck and deeply gouged modelling on the lower half of the body of the pot are very well balanced. The impressed pattern on the surface surrounding the gouged curves is probably made with a metal ring.

PLATE LXXIV. POTTERY DESIGN

Top left: Black earthenware pot with moulded decoration. No documentation. (?) Zulu. S. Africa. British Museum.—
The regular bands of moulded pellets on this pot form an interesting contrast to the more angular knobs used in the next
illustration. Their arrangement on the body of the pot is excellent.

Top right: Earthenware pot with moulded decoration. No documentation. Congo, Musée Royal de l'Afrique Centrale.—The
decoration on the upper half of the body of this pot is much more roughly executed than that of the previous one, but the
total effect has a vitality which the other lacks.

Bottom left: Earthenware pot splashed with vegetable matter. Height 32 cm. Sundi or related tribe. Lower Congo. Musée
Royal de l'Afrique Centrale.—Both from the point of view of its general shape and its decoration this is a very beautiful pot;
the basic colour is a very pale pinkish biscuit, and the splashed pattern is in several shades of brown.

Bottom right: Painted earthenware pot. Height 30 cm. Provenance, Stanley Pool. Probably Teke tribe. Lower Congo.
Musée Royal de l'Afrique Centrale.—The body of this pot is roughly painted in vandyke brown.

PLATE LXXV. POTTERY DESIGN

Earthenware pot. Ashanti tribe. Ghana. British Museum.—This ceremonial pot which was used to contain the wine poured upon the Golden Stool has a very fine design which can also be seen on the gold Soul-Bearer's disc illustrated in Plate LXVII (*bottom right*).

PLATE LXXVI. POTTERY DESIGN

Top left: Encased pot. Height 20 cm. Angba tribe. Uele. Congo. Musée Royal de l'Afrique Centrale.—The neck and base of this pot are encased with a woven fibre covering which is continued as a handle. The body has a decorative binding of strips of cane framing small panels which show roulette decoration.

Top right: Encased pot. Height 32 cm. Bali tribe. Uele. Congo. Musée Royal de l'Afrique Centrale.—The whole pot is encased in a fibre covering which in itself is a beautifully decorative piece of work.

Bottom, left and right: Cow dung pots. Provenance, Kadero. Nuba Hills. Kordofan. British Museum.—These two bowls which are made of cow dung are painted in white and red earth on the dark brown surface and are excellent examples of rich, freely painted design on pottery.